THE Original BIG BOOK OF PENCIL PASTIMES®

THE Original BIG BOOK OF PENCIL® PASTIMES

By James F. Minter

Bristol Park Books

First Bristol Park Books edition published in 1993.
New edition published in 2003.

Bristol Park Books, Inc.
450 Raritan Center Parkway
Edison, NJ 08837

Pencil Pastimes is a registered trademark of Bristol Park Books, Inc.
Bristol Park Books is a registered trademark of Bristol Park Books, Inc.

Published by arrangement with Hart Associates.

ISBN: 0-88486-313-1

Printed in the United States of America.

Contents

5

Body English

Below, you will find 40 familiar expressions or titles, each containing an anatomical reference. Fill in each blank with the name of the missing part of the body; for example, You go to my *head*.

   A score of 29 is run-of-the-mill; 34 is good; and 39 is superb.

 1. All _____ on deck

 2. The _____ of Darkness

 3. Rings on her _____, bells on her _____

 4. I've got you under my _____

 5. Mine _____ have seen the glory

 6. By the skin of our _____

 7. Little pitchers have big _____

 8. A stiff upper _____

 9. _____ of clay

10. Keep your _____ up

11. A well-turned _____

12. Don't stick your _____ out

13. _____ grease

14. Was this the _____ that launched a thousand ships?

15. _____ in cheek

16. A lump in the _____

17. Rule of _____

18. Pot _____ stove

8

19. Out on a _____

20. _____ Diamond

21. The long _____ of the law

22. Community _____

23. The Golden _____

24. Put your head on my _____

25. _____ of the dog

26. By the hair of my _____-_____

   _____

27. Barefoot boy with _____ of tan

28. A _____ for news

29. Rule with an iron _____

30. An iron _____ (medical device)

31. Cod _____ oil

32. A _____ watch

33. Steak and _____ pie

34. Tough as _____

35. Nothing but skin and _____

36. Filet of _____

37. A cigarette _____

38. The Iron _____ (Jack London novel)

39. Fighting _____ and nail

40. The way to a man's _____ is

   through his _____

On Ice

Below, you will find 32 words and expressions. Each one should suggest to you another expression which contains the three letters I-C-E. The dashes indicate missing letters. For example, *gaming cubes* are *d*ICE.

A score of 18 is fair; 25 is very good; 30 ices the cake.

1. __ ICE   Vermin

2. ICE __ __ __ __   Nation in North Atlantic

3. __ __ ICE __ __ __ __ __ __ __   Dinosaur

4. __ __ ICE __ __
    __ __ __ __ __ __ __ __ __ __   Lewis Carroll favorite

5. __ ICE __ __   Finer point

6. __ ICE   Food staple

7. __ ICE __ __ __ __ __ __ __ __ __   Second in command

8. __ __ __ ICE __ __ __
    __ __ __   John Steinbeck novel

9. __ __ ICE   Flavoring

10. __ __ ICE   Cost

11. ICE __ __ __ __   Floe

12. __ __ ICE   Instant

13. __ __ __ __ __ __ __ __ ICE   To put at ease

14. __ ICE __ __ __ __ __ __ __ __   200th birthday

15. _ ICE _ _ _   Official permission

16. _ _ _ ICE _ _ _

    _ _ _ _ _ _   Eugene O'Neill play

17. _ _ _ ICE   Mechanical contraption

18. _ _ ICE _ _   Muscle of upper arm

19. ICE _ _ _ _ _ _ _   Winter sport

20. _ _ _ _ _ ICE   Black candy

21. _ _ ICE   Sliver

22. _ _ _ ICE   Option

23. _ _ _ _ _ _ ICE   Cliff

24. _ ICE   City in the South of France

25. _ ICE _ _ _ _ _   Police division

26. _ _ _ ICE   Counsel

27. _ _ _ ICE   Lure

28. _ _ _ ICE _ _   Seldom speaking

29. _ _ ICE _ _ _ _   Invaluable; irreplaceable

30. _ _ _ _ _ _ _ _ _ _ _ ICE   Met diva from Mississippi

31. _ ICE _ _ _ _ _ _   Lascivious

32. _ _ _ _ _ ICE _ _

    _ _ _ _ _ _ _ _ _   Play by van Druten

11

A Run for Your Money

Below, you will find 20 expressions or definitions. Each one of these should suggest a word or an expression which contains the word RUN. For example, *a person who comes in second in a contest* is a RUNner-up.

A score of 11 is fine; 14 is superior; and 17 is exceptional.

1. Youth who leaves home and disappears _____
2. Site of Civil War battle _____
3. A try-out _____
4. Eventually; in the course of time _____
5. Film directed by and starring Woody Allen _____
6. In poor condition _____
7. Special fork of "The Owl and the Pussycat" fame _____
8. To meet unexpectedly _____
9. Ordinary; average _____
10. To go through an ordeal at many hands; Indian physical trial _____
11. A light motorboat or car _____
12. Four-base hit _____
13. Have a fever _____
14. Show marked superiority over _____
15. To come to an end of; to exhaust _____
16. Where planes take off and land _____
17. A late breakfast; combination of first meal and mid-day meal _____
18. Author of "guys and dolls" stories _____
19. Predecessor or precursor _____
20. Where the Magna Charta is said to have been signed _____

12

The Night Game

Below, you will find 21 words, phrases, and expressions. Each should suggest a word or an expression which contains the word NIGHT. For example, *a frightening dream* is a NIGHTmare.

A score of 12 is average; 14 is good; and 18 is outstanding.

1. Shady; irresponsible; transitory _____
2. 1967 film starring Rod Steiger and Sidney Poitier _____
3. Garment designed for wear in bed _____
4. A person who stays up late _____
5. Benevolent fraternity _____
6. English nurse known as "The Lady with the Lamp" _____
7. Beatle film and album _____
8. Stopover; single performance _____
9. Eugene O'Neill play _____
10. Shakespeare comedy featuring Sir Toby Belch _____
11. F. Scott Fitzgerald novel _____
12. Famous Rembrandt painting _____
13. Restaurant open after dark, with music and dancing _____
14. Popular Yuletide poem _____
15. Drink taken at bedtime _____
16. Shakespeare comedy featuring Puck _____
17. Tennessee Williams play _____
18. Musical by Stephen Sondheim _____
19. Belladonna _____
20. The tales of Scheherazade _____
21. Narrative poem by Longfellow _____

We'll Give You a Cue

Using the 27 definitions below, fill in the blanks. Each answer begins with the letter Q and contains five letters.

If you get 14 correct answers, you are doing fine; 17 is particularly good; 21 is excellent; and 24 rates you tops.

1. Fraudulent doctor   Q _ _ _ _

2. Feminine ruler   Q _ _ _ _

3. Peculiarity in manner or behavior   Q _ _ _ _

4. Swift; rapid   Q _ _ _ _

5. Tranquil; still   Q _ _ _ _

6. Search, seek   Q _ _ _ _

7. Completely; very   Q _ _ _ _

8. Seemingly; as if; almost   Q _ _ _ _

9. To drink freely   Q _ _ _ _

10. Strange; eccentric   Q _ _ _ _

11. A game bird; to cower   Q _ _ _ _

12. To cite; adduce; repeat   Q _ _ _ _

13. Proportional part or share   Q _ _ _ _

14. Two pints   Q _ _ _ _

15. Feather   Q _ _ _ _

16. Said; spoke   Q _ _ _ _

17. A question   Q _ _ _ _

18. Misgiving; apprehension   Q _ _ _ _

19. Coverlet   Q _ _ _ _

20. Overpower; suppress; soothe   Q _ _ _ _

21. To annul; make void   Q _ _ _ _

22. Shiver   Q _ _ _ _

23. Pigtail; waiting line   Q _ _ _ _

24. A quantity of paper   Q _ _ _ _

25. A discus; a circle of rope   Q _ _ _ _

26. Bargeman's pole   Q _ _ _ _

27. Handmill for grinding corn   Q _ _ _ _

The Little Things

Below, you will find 40 familiar expressions, each containing the word LITTLE. Fill in each blank with the appropriate word or phrase which completes the expression.

A score of 20 is fair; 25, good; 30, excellent; and 35, splendid!

1. Little Miss _____
2. Try a little _____
3. In my little corner of _____
4. A little bit of _____
5. Little things mean _____
6. Hush, little baby, don't _____
7. It only _____ for a little while
8. A little learning is a _____
9. Where oh where has my little _____ gone?
10. Little _____ Annie
11. Little _____, Arkansas
12. I'm called Little _____
13. Every little movement has a meaning all _____
14. Say a little _____ for me
15. Daddy's little _____
16. Those little white _____
17. Suffer the little _____ to come unto me
18. Little Big _____
19. Mighty oaks from little _____ grow

16

20. My little brown _____

21. And a little child shall _____ them

22. There was a little girl and she had a little _____

23. O Little Town of _____

24. Little strokes fell great _____

25. Little _____ have big ears

26. Little old _____

27. Mary had a little _____

28. Little boys are made of _____ and _____

29. The fog comes on little _____

30. Thank Heaven for Little _____

31. Eliza _____ little

32. Little boats should keep _____

33. Little Boy Blue, come blow _____

34. Little _____ sat in a corner

35. Little _____, who made thee?

36. A little _____ and soon hot

37. Men who _____ much say little

38. You gotta _____ a little, _____ a little, let

    your _____ a little

39. Little _____ has lost her sheep

40. He is always a _____ who cannot live on little

Sound-alike Pairs

Below, you will find 28 sentences. Each of these sentences is to be completed with a pair of homonyms (two words that sound identical but are spelled differently). For example, *When he saw the unadorned jet he said: "This is a* PLAIN PLANE.*"*

A score of 10 is fair; 17 is good; and 22 is outstanding.

1. Cyrano's proboscis is wise. His   _____   _____
2. Some cities have an equitable
   transportation fee, or a   _____   _____
3. My barbecue turns out superb
   burgers. It's a   _____   _____
4. Dad will have a couple of those
   pens, and give Mom   _____   _____
5. I had four cookies, and John
   had twice as many. He   _____   _____
6. That chicken is not fit for man
   or beast. It's a   _____   _____
7. My bucket faded in the sun.
   It's a   _____   _____
8. I looked through every drawer
   of that desk and I can't find my
   crayons. Are you sure   _____   _____
9. When he saw that his bill
   totaled $10,000 he exclaimed,
   "That is   _____   _____
10. Keep your voice down to a
    whisper. There is no talking   _____   _____
11. Phillip never seems to get
    enough to eat. You just can't   _____   _____

12. Mom became a swinger, but dignified Dad _____ _____

13. When we go boating with the girls, Ann paddles and _____ _____

14. Aunt Liz is as old as the hills. There's hardly anything _____ _____

15. These daisies are edible. They're made of _____ _____

16. Ben is a prison contractor. He _____ _____

17. He's a waiter on an ocean liner. He belongs to one of the _____ _____

18. The robber hid the money in a _____ _____

19. Those letters are meant for men's eyes only. They're strictly _____ _____

20. That fishing pole is only a kid's toy, but mine is a _____ _____

21. He performed the wrong ceremony. It wasn't the _____ _____

22. I can *see* the show fine from where I sit, but I can't _____ _____

23. They poured ink into the chimney and it _____ _____

24. He never smiles. He has a _____ _____

25. That mare has laryngitis. She's a _____ _____

26. The head of our school explained the school's philosophy of education. He is a _____ _____

27. The antelope has given birth. The zoo now has a _____ _____

28. Pete is only an amateur writer, but Jill and Larry are _____ _____

19

Take It to Heart

The 25 definitions below should each suggest an expression which contains the word HEART. For example, *Enthusiastic or invigorating* is HEARTY.

A score of 13 is fair; 16 is above average; and 20 is superlative.

1. What happens when you're excited   _____
2. Area of political importance   _____
3. Anguish; sorrow   _____
4. Pleasantly moving or stirring   _____
5. Novel by Nathanael West   _____
6. Area in front of a fireplace   _____
7. Coronary thrombosis   _____
8. Sincere, frank discussion   _____
9. Causing intense grief, anguish, or pain   _____
10. To commit to memory   _____
11. Tony Bennett recording   _____
12. Operation pioneered by Dr. Christiaan Barnard   _____
13. Edgar Allan Poe short story   _____
14. Song from *Damn Yankees*   _____
15. Generous and kindly   _____
16. Beatle recording   _____
17. Discourage; depress   _____
18. To envy or regret deeply   _____
19. Movie based on novel by Carson McCullers   _____
20. Show one's feelings   _____
21. Graham Greene novel   _____
22. Ailment caused by excess stomach acid   _____
23. Novel by Joseph Conrad, set in Africa   _____
24. Oscar-winning documentary on Vietnam   _____
25. Fraternity song   _____

No Holds Barred

Each one of these 23 definitions should suggest a word or phrase which contains the word BAR. For example, an argument in a baseball game is a rhuBARb

A score of 11 is average; 15 is excellent; 17 is extraordinary.

1. Star of *Funny Girl* _____
2. Primitive; savage; uncivilized _____
3. Bonnie and Clyde's gang _____
4. Outdoor cooking _____
5. Sentimental male singing group _____
6. Drug taken to induce sleep _____
7. Well-known English financial institution _____
8. William Shakespeare _____
9. Voracious giant fish of southern waters _____
10. Grain used for liquor, cereal _____
11. Person who serves drinks _____
12. Nickname for Frederick I _____
13. To begin on a journey _____
14. Robber released by Pontius Pilate instead of Jesus _____
15. To discomfit or disconcert _____
16. Someone fond of luxury and pleasure _____
17. Red-light district in San Francisco _____
18. Female founder of the Red Cross _____
19. Iron or steel tool used as a pry _____
20. Eject from the lawyers' association _____
21. Restriction on trade _____
22. Strolling player _____
23. Daredevil pilot's maneuver _____

Moongazing

Below, you will find 24 definitions. Each should suggest an expression which contains the word MOON. For example, *A vacation by newlyweds* is a honeyMOON.

A score of 12 is fair; 16 is superior; and 20 is stupendous.

1. Movie starring Betty Grable   _____
2. Well-known Beethoven work   _____
3. Song by Henry Mancini   _____
4. Comic strip character   _____
5. Henry Hudson's ship   _____
6. Song by Rogers and Hart   _____
7. Very infrequently   _____
8. American labor leader   _____
9. Illegally distilled corn whiskey   _____
10. Movie starring Marlon Brando   _____
11. Head of Unification Church   _____
12. Hold two jobs at once   _____
13. Play by Eugene O'Neill   _____
14. Detective novel by Wilkie Collins   _____
15. Novel by Somerset Maugham   _____
16. Novel by Jules Verne   _____
17. Song by Glenn Miller   _____
18. Fancied celestial face   _____
19. Walt Disney movie   _____
20. Movie starring Ryan O'Neal; song of the 1930's   _____
21. Bossa nova hit of the 1960's   _____
22. Foolish or absent-minded person   _____
23. Go for broke at hearts   _____
24. Complaining futilely   _____

About Face

Each of the 24 definitions below should suggest to you an expression which contains the word FACE. For example, *Lacking individuality* is FACEless.

A score of 16 is fine; 19 is superior; and 22 is exceptional.

1. Disfigure; mar _____
2. Unconcealed; shameless _____
3. De-aging process _____
4. One aspect _____
5. Eradicate _____
6. Confront an unpleasant situation _____
7. Witty; given to levity _____
8. Introduction _____
9. Nickname of Al Capone _____
10. Embarrassed _____
11. Exterior _____
12. Double-dealing; ambiguous _____
13. Heavy print _____
14. To look sad, sullen _____
15. Confronting closely _____
16. Apparent worth _____
17. Term in hockey _____
18. Preserve one's reputation _____
19. Indian term for white settlers _____
20. Type of wristwatch or sandwich _____
21. Poem by John Henry Titus _____
22. Oscar-winning film for Joanne Woodward _____
23. Former Pittsburgh Pirate relief pitcher _____
24. Ingmar Bergman film _____

Eat, Drink, and Be Merry

Here are 40 expressions, song or story titles, each of which contains the name of some food or drink. How many goodies can you fill in?

A score of 25 is just peachy; 30 is top banana; and 35 or more is the cream of the crop.

1. The _____ is as high as an elephant's eye

2. _____ of human kindness

3. Yes, we have no _____

4. The queen of hearts, she ate some _____

5. _____ hill

6. _____ house of the August moon

7. Of _____ and kings

8. You can catch more flies with _____

   than with _____

9. _____ in the straw

10. _____ are jumpin' and the cotton is high

11. _____ and roses

12. Slower than _____

13. _____'s Peak

14. Partridge in a _____ tree

15. In the shade of the old _____ tree

16. Mrs. Murphy's _____

17. _____ barrel polka

18. Don't put all your _____ in one basket

19. That won't cut the _____

20. _____ of the crop

21. _____ 'n' _____ 'n' everything nice

22. _____ loaf Mountain

23. _____ in the sky

24. To _____ in your own juice

25. Land of _____ and _____

26. Jack and the _____ stalk

27. _____ tree, very pretty

28. Red as a _____

29. _____ drum

30. Buy me some _____ and _____

31. The princess and the _____

32. Under the spreading _____ tree

33. The _____ of wrath

34. _____ boats are comin'

35. He stuck in his thumb and pulled out a _____

36. Georgia _____

37. _____ Little

38. You're the cream in my _____

39. A jug of _____, a loaf of _____, and thou

40. The moon is made of green _____

The Name of the Dame

Below you will find titles or lines from 44 songs, novels, movies, or plays. One element is missing in each—the first name of the famed dame. Can you fill in the blanks?

A score of 25 is good; 30 is superior; and 40 is phenomenal.

1. _____ o' My Heart

2. When You and I Were Young, _____

3. Sweet _____ Malone

4. _____ I Dream of Lilac Time

5. _____ in the Sky with Diamonds

6. Kiss Me, _____

7. Little _____ Rooney

8. _____ Dobson

9. _____ and Abelard

10. _____ of the Crossways

11. Antony and _____

12. Good, Night, _____

13. _____ in Wonderland

14. Every little breeze seems to whisper _____

15. If You Knew _____

16. _____ Karenina

17. _____ and Clyde

18. Hello, _____

19. _____ Marlene

26

20. Come, _____, in My Flying Machine

21. My Friend _____

22. _____ Rigby

23. _____ Is a Grand Old Name

24. _____ Pierce

25. I love all the charms about _____

26. _____ Dallas

27. _____ of Washington Square

28. Perils of _____

29. I Dream of _____ with the Light Brown Hair

30. Sioux City _____

31. My Sister _____

32. _____ Miller

33. _____ Grandet

34. Who's Afraid of _____ Woolf?

35. Song of _____

36. _____ Gabler

37. _____ Eyre

38. Sister _____

39. _____ Foyle

40. All About _____

41. _____ Doone

42. My Night at _____'s

43. _____ Lescaut

44. _____ of the Spirits

Around the House

Complete each expression by filling in the blank with the name of a household item; for example, Sweep the dirt under the *rug*.

A score of 25 is good; 32, superb; and if you score a perfect 40, you must be a perfect housekeeper.

1. Just _____ it over

2. A new _____ sweeps clean

3. You turned the _____ on me

4. Skeleton in the _____

5. All alone by the _____

6. Home on the _____

7. Everything but the _____

8. _____, Iowa

9. The _____ calls the _____ black

10. Little _____ have big ears

11. _____, _____, on the wall

12. Out of the _____ and into the fire

13. Blue-_____ special

14. Rub-a-dub-dub, three men in a _____

15. _____ of Vital Statistics

16. Born with a silver _____

17. Strike while the _____ is hot

18. Oil for the _____ of China

19. Bring down the _____

28

20. Life is just a _____ of cherries

21. _____ the meeting

22. _____ the discussion

23. The _____ was bare

24. Her life is no _____ of roses

25. Bell, Book and _____

26. The _____ ran away with the spoon.

27. You _____ yourself too thin.

28. My _____ runneth over.

29. Tempest in a _____

30. A Geiger _____

31. The President and his _____

32. Nature abhors a _____

33. *Once upon a* _____

34. Butcher, baker, _____ maker

35. *Through the Looking* _____

36. _____ City Music Hall

38. *The* _____*'s Edge*

38. The silver _____

39. Katy, bar the _____

40. The mouse ran up the _____

Play Your Card

Below are 20 definitions, each of which should suggest a word or phrase that contains the letters CARD. For example, *objects used in bridge, poker, rummy, etc.* are playing CARDS.

A score of 12 is good enough for openers; 15 entitles you to a raise; 18 takes the pot.

1. Instrument that registers heart movement   _____

2. Decorative indicator of where a guest should sit   _____

3. In rummy, the opposite of draw   _____

4. Bird; church VIP   _____

5. Be frank; tell the whole story   _____

6. Library file   _____

7. Well-known brand of rum   _____

8. Cessation of heartbeat   _____

9. Poster; public notice   _____

10. Thistlelike plant related to artichoke   _____

11. Jack, queen or king   _____

12. Businessperson's identification   _____

13. Supreme Court successor to O.W. Holmes   _____

14. National League baseball team   _____

15. Herb or spice   _____

16. Capital of Wales; coal-shipping port   _____

17. Style of sweater   _____

18. One who wins at cards by cheating   _____

19. Character played by Desi Arnaz   _____

20. President of France   _____

Horsing Around

Below, you will find 15 definitions. Each should suggest an expression that contains the word HORSE. For example, *to flog* is HORSEwhip.

A score of 9 is not bad; 11 is above average; and 14 means you have a lot of horse sense.

1. 1932 Marx Brothers movie   _____

2. Trade offered by Richard III at Bosworth Field; famous quote from Shakespeare's *Richard III*, V, iv, 7   _____

3. National symbol of the Saxons; a popular brand of Scotch   _____

4. A separate matter; something entirely distinct   _____

5. Derisive response to early automobile drivers   _____

6. Reprimand advising one not to question favors   _____

7. 1969 Jane Fonda movie about dance marathons during the Depression   _____

8. Gymnastics apparatus used for vaulting   _____

9. Mask; pretense; pretext   _____

10. Person undertaking arduous labor   _____

11. Insect   _____

12. Nut-producing tree; a shade of brown   _____

13. An unknown; in politics, a candidate unexpectedly nominated   _____

14. Colossal figure used by the ancient Greeks as a strategem of war   _____

15. Early name for cars   _____

Puns for Fun

Each of the 33 sentences below contains a blank line that represents a missing word. Following this blank line is a word in parentheses. This word and the missing word sound exactly alike, *but are spelled different-ly*. It's up to you to fill in the correct homonym in the space provided.

For example, the incomplete sentence, *Our cleaning is done by a _____ (made)* would be completed with the word MAID.

A score of 20 is good; 25 is very good; and 30 or more is "caws" for joy.

1. The boys spent the night in a _____ (*hostile*).

2. He stood on the rostrum and _____ (*invade*) against the preceding speaker.

3. The Honolulu welcoming committee presented him with a _____ (*lay*).

4. The expedition picked up a good deal of moss and _____ (*likens*).

5. They began to _____ (*martial*) all their forces.

6. A small _____ (*cleek*) dominated the meeting.

7. On the lake floated a duck and a _____ (*signet*).

8. Character is written into one's _____ (*jeans*).

9. His foot caught in a _____ (*fisher*) in the rock.

10. To spruce up and feel spry, _____ (*flecks*) your muscles.

11. "There is no _____ (*bomb*) in Gilead," cried the prophet.

12. The Indian maharajah conversed with the Turkish _____ (*bay*).

13. "You are a lout and a _____ (*nave*)," he shouted.

14. Every human eye has a tear _____ (*ducked*).

15. The Japanese _____ (*ewe*) is a splendid conifer.

16. The treasure constituted a _____ (*cash*) of great value.

17. The cow pasture was full of _____ (*awful*).

18. A _____ (*bolder*) crashed down the mountainside.

19. It's easy to _____ (*cousin*) the unsuspecting.

20. He knew what to say, but didn't know how to _____ (*frays*) it.

21. The students _____ (*hide*) home from school.

22. An ornamented _____ (*freeze*) adorned the temple.

23. She tied her hair in a beautiful _____ (*plate*).

24. After the third litter, Sally had her cat _____ (*spade*).

25. Sitting Bull was a leader of the _____ (*sue*) tribe.

26. My horse strayed from the _____ (*bridal*) path.

27. The failing mark on his report card did not _____ (*phase*) him in the least.

28. The thief _____ (*rood*) his crime.

29. The bank manager will surely _____ (*nicks*) Bill's loan request.

30. Every mother bird cares for her _____ (*brewed*).

31. The lion fought with might and _____ (*mane*).

32. Her coat was made of _____ (*links*).

33. By your pupils you'll be _____ (*taut*).

Fanfare

Below are 25 clues. Each one of these should suggest to you an expression which contains the three letters FAN. The dashes correspond to the letters that are missing. For example, *illusionary or whimsical* is FAN*ciful*.

If you get 13 right, you're doing fine; 17 is excellent; and 20 is an outstanding score.

1. FAN _ _ _ _ _   Lively Spanish dance

2. FAN _ _ _ _ _ _   Without amorous at-
                            tachment

3. _ _ _ _ _ FAN _   Jack London novel

4. FAN _ _ _ _ _ _ _ _   Noted Boston building

5. FAN _ _ _ _   Letters sent to celebri-
                            ties

6. _ _ FAN _   Newborn baby

7. FAN _ _ _ _ _ _   John Cleland novel

8. _ _ _ _ _ _ _ _ _ _ _ _

    FAN _ _ _ _ _ _   To dance

9. FAN _ _ _ _   Imagination; hallucina-
                            tion

10. FAN _ _ _ _   Exhibiting excessive en-
                            thusiasm

34

11. FAN __ __   __ __ __ __ __   "Funny Girl" heroine

12. __ __ FAN __ __ __   Foot soldiers

13. FAN - __ __ __ __   Chinese gambling game

14. FAN   __ __ __   __ __ __ __ __ __   Incite

15. __ __ __ FAN __   Secular; impure; irrev-
                                           erent

16. FAN __ __ __ __ __ __ __ __   Long-running New
                                           York musical

17. FAN __ __ __ __ __   Disney movie

18. __ __ __ __   FAN   __ __ __ __ __   Mozart opera

19. FAN __ __ __ __ __ __   __ __ __ __ __ __   Science fiction movie of
                                           1960's

20. FAN __ __ __ __   Chair style

21. __ __ __ FAN __ __ __ __   How old-timers
                                           describe new ideas

22. __ __ __ FAN __   Famous stained-glass
                                           lamp

23. __ __ FAN __ __ __ __ __ __ __ __ __   Unmanageable,
                                           troublesome child

24. __ __ __ FAN __ __ __ __ __ __ __   Strong medication for
                                           venereal diseases

25. __ __ __ __ FAN __   Puffed out

Mother Lode

Below, you will find 28 definitions, each of which identifies a word which contains the letters O R E. The dashes correspond to the letters that are missing. For example, *a seasoning* is OREgano.

If you get 14 right, you're doing fine; 18 is excellent; and 23 is an outstanding scORE.

1. _ _ _ _ ORE   Beseech

2. _ _ _ _ _ _ ORE   Person who loads ships

3. _ _ _ ORE   Plentiful; abundant

4. _ _ _ ORE   City in Pakistan

5. _ _ ORE   Land bordering a body of
                                   water

6. _ _ _ _ _ _ ORE   Type of code; signal

7. _ _ ORE _ _ _ _ _ _ _ _   Stated previously

8. ORE _ _ _   Famous Western trail

9. _ _ _ _ _ _ ORE   Southeast Asian city

10. _ _ _ _ _ _ _ ORE   Hitherto

11. _ _ ORE   Love; worship

12. ORE _ _   Mountain nymph

13. _ _ ORE   Minute reproductive body of a plant

14. ORE _ _ _ _   Figure in Greek mythology; son of Agamemnon

15. _ _ ORE   Breathe hoarsely during sleep

16. _ _ _ _ ORE   Regret; lament

17. _ ORE _   Fixed customs of a group

18. _ _ ORE   Took an oath

19. _ _ _ _ ORE   Investigate

20. _ _ ORE   Routine task

21. _ _ _ ORE _ _   Living in trees

22. _ ORE _ _ _ _   Bullfighter

23. _ _ _ _ ORE   Disagreeable sight

24. _ _ _ ORE _ _ _ _ _ _ _   Planting of new trees

25. _ ORE _ _ _ _ _ _ _ _ _ _   A person of the same faith

26. _ ORE _ _ _   Alien; from another country

27. _ _ ORE _ _ _ _ _ _ _ _   Ballet creator

28. _ _ _ _ _ _ ORE   Insect eating plant

Rhyming Expressions

Below are definitions for 45 words or expressions which are composed of rhyming syllables. Can you supply the answers? Example: a *Chinese gambling game* is FAN-TAN.

A score of 25 is good; 30 proclaims you a poet; 40 is superduper.

1. Dumbbell; vehicle riding empty   _____
2. TV set   _____
3. Card game; bludgeon   _____
4. Candied fruit and the like   _____
5. Barrel organ   _____
6. Trash; stuff and nonsense   _____
7. Helplessly; by compulsion   _____
8. Show-off; skillful, aggressive performer   _____
9. Guileful trickery; illicit amour   _____
10. Disorderly confusion; Beatles song made infamous by Charles Manson   _____
11. Ice cream flavor containing candied fruit   _____
12. Lavish party; spree   _____
13. Sinuous, suggestive carnival dance   _____
14. Derisive term for large political contributor   _____
15. Magic incantation   _____
16. Ritualistic gibberish   _____
17. The masses (Greek)   _____
18. Fussbudget; stuffed shirt   _____
19. Insipid; unmanly   _____
20. Heedlessly; (with different spelling) Presley film   _____

21. To show obsequious deference; fawn _____

22. Deterioration through use _____

23. Indiscriminately; headlong _____

24. Pal around with; chat with _____

25. Expletive; opener of a song extolling a young lady's eyes _____

26. Cheap dance hall; part of a Rolling Stones song title _____

27. Precursor of stereo recording _____

28. What the big bad wolf threatened to do _____

29. Haitian black magic _____

30. Noisy confusion of sound; excitement _____

31. A stew of various ingredients; mixture _____

32. Slang superlative of the 1920's _____

33. Close relatives and friends _____

34. Very loyal _____

35. Completely just and honorable _____

36. Promise of utopian fulfillment _____

37. Eighty _____

38. The jitters _____

39. Simple, unpretentious girl _____

40. Best TV viewing slot _____

41. The London press _____

42. The sound of crying _____

43. Nocturnal rendezvous _____

44. When air fare is often cheaper _____

45. Labor holiday _____

What's in a Word?

How many of the following words can you define? A good score is 12; 16 is excellent; 19 makes you a lexicographer.

1. EUPHORIA
   Fear
   Joy
   Misery
   Delicacy

2. INTRANSIGENT
   Vagabond
   Moving
   Uncompromising
   Fluid

3. MARPLOT
   Parrot
   Meddler
   Conspiracy
   Building site

4. NESCIENCE
   Ignorance
   Occult
   Foresight
   Enemy

5. BANAL
   Bathtub
   Trite
   Absurd
   Sturdy

6. MISANTHROPE
   Hater of mankind
   Hater of women
   Lover of mankind
   Lover of women

7. PERQUISITE
   Private
   Prism
   Prizefighter
   Privilege

8. PETULANT
   Annoying
   Searching
   Irritable
   Ludicrous

9. SATRAP
   Snare
   Ornament
   Subordinate ruler
   Strike

10. SOLON
    Legislator   Aria
    Party   Statue

11. DRACONIAN
    Extreme   Dragon-like
    Contradictory   Slow

12. PLATITUDE
    Commonplace remark Flatness
    Width   Beauty

13. APOCRYPHAL
    Of doubtful authenticity   Senseless
    Speechless   Inevitable

14. EXTROVERTED
    Stubborn   Ornery
    Outgoing   Expelled

15. UMBRAGE
    Resentment   Parasol
    Patronage   Undergrowth

16. EXACERBATE
    Puzzle   Fortify
    Aggravate   Diminish

17. FINAGLE
    Baby eagle   Trifle
    Wangle   Harpoon

18. CASTIGATE
    Iron fence   Punish
    Gratify   Reward

19. ANATHEMA
    Ban   Peninsula
    Wheezing   Splendor

20. ROCOCO
    Lavishly ornate   Stony
    Breakfast table   Barren

The Story of Man

Below are 38 clues. Each should suggest a word or expression which contains the letters MAN. For example, *a raving lunatic* is a MANiac.

A score of 20 is okay; 27 is pretty good; and 23—MANy congratulations!

1. Most important of New York's five boroughs _____

2. An aperture in the pavement through which workers enter _____

3. Rudyard Kipling story made into a film starring Michael Caine and Sean Connery _____

4. A large West African baboon _____

5. To have fingernails trimmed and polished _____

6. Black magic _____

7. A facing of stone, wood, or marble above the fireplace _____

8. Food miraculously provided for the Israelites in the desert _____

9. Scold severely; rebuke _____

10. 1960's film about Thomas More's conflict with King Henry VIII _____

11. Public official under the Chinese empire _____

12. Stringed musical instrument similar to a lute _____

13. Author of *The Magic Mountain* and *Death in Venice* _____

14. Required; obligatory _____

15. Famous race horse _____

16. Supervisor of a construction crew _____
17. Constituents' wishes expressed through an election _____
18. Specially trained soldier; shock trooper _____
19. Public declaration of policy or opinion _____
20. Speech in which Abraham Lincoln freed the slaves _____
21. Metallic element used in making glass, paint, medicine _____
22. Handcuffs _____
23. Director or administrator _____
24. Spanish veil or scarf worn by women _____
25. Short story by Edward Everett Hale _____
26. Small explanatory book or pamphlet _____
27. Unprinted book or paper, typed or handwritten _____
28. Factory owner or one who produces goods _____
29. Indian tribe, now in Oklahoma _____
30. Largest city in the Philippines _____
31. Birthplace of Virgil in Italy _____
32. Edward VIII's famous reference to Wallis Simpson _____
33. Waste products of animals; also fertilizer _____
34. Clothing model in store windows _____
35. Large industrial city in Lancashire, England _____
36. Use someone skillfully to one's own advantage _____
37. Secretary _____
38. Study of word meanings _____

Of THEE I Sing

Below are 30 clues, each of which should suggest a word or phrase containing the letters T H E. See how many you can provide.

A score of 20 is good; 24 is excellent; 26 makes you the cream of the crop.

1. Instrument to indicate temperature   THE _ _ _ _ _ _ _

2. Greek letter   THE _ _

3. Flat stringed instrument   _ _ THE _

4. Sad; pitiable   _ _ THE _ _ _

5. Margaret Mitchell novel of 1936   _ _ _ _   _ _ _ _

        THE   _ _ _ _

6. Larceny   THE _ _

7. Bird's coat   _ _ _ THE _ _

8. Machine for turning something   _ _ THE

9. Cinema or playhouse   THE _ _ _ _

10. Husband of Desdemona; Shakespeare play   _ THE _ _ _

11. Wash oneself   _ _ THE

12. Topic; written composition   THE _ _

13. Actor   THE _ _ _ _ _

14. Oedipus' city   THE _ _ _

15. Study of religion   THE _ _ _ _ _

16. Pagan; uncivilized   _ _ _ THE _

17. Animal skin   _ _ _ THE _

18. Bounteous giver   _ _ THE _   _ _ _ _ _ _

19. One of Christ's 12 apostles   _ _ _ THE _

20. Algebra, geometry, etc.   _ _ THE _ _ _ _ _

21. 1941 Noel Coward comedy   _ _ _ THE   _ _ _ _ _ _

22. Capital of Greece   _ THE _ _

23. Boil; be furious   _ _ _ THE

24. Despise   _ _ _THE

25. Supposition; speculation   THE _ _ _

26. Curved harvesting implement   _ _ _THE

27. Jar for storing hot or cold liquids   THE _ _ _ _

28. O'Neill masterpiece of 1946   THE   _ _ _ _ _ _

      _ _ _ _ _ _

29. Tsarina with strange tastes   _ _ THE _ _ _ _

30. Squirm; twist oneself in pain   _ _ _THE

Double Trouble

Below are 35 pairs of definitions. The correct answer to the first definition of each pair, minus its first letter, will yield the correct answer to the second definition of that pair. For example:

Bird, usually black in color: CROW
Column: ROW

A score of 20 correct pairs is fair; 25 is very good; and 30 is extraordinary.

1. Take care of
   Finale
   _____
   _____

2. Gulp
   Sprawl or roll in
   _____
   _____

3. Woodland path
   Metal bar
   _____
   _____

4. Hoofed animal
   Cereal grain
   _____
   _____

5. Carry
   Sensory organ
   _____
   _____

6. Game bird
   Awaken
   _____
   _____

7. Wild pig
   Rowing device
   _____
   _____

8. Small woodland animal
   Stand for painting
   _____
   _____

9. Citrus fruit
   Grazing area
   _____
   _____

10. Semiprecious stone   _____
    Entranceway   _____

11. Bone's core   _____
    Tell's projectile   _____

12. Animal classification   _____
    Swamp grass   _____

13. Festival   _____
    Atmosphere   _____

14. Games   _____
    Havens for ships   _____

15. Streetcar   _____
    Male sheep   _____

16. Wagon   _____
    Skill   _____

17. Follow   _____
    Display stand   _____

18. Retain   _____
    Ancient   _____

19. Monk's garb   _____
    Nocturnal bird   _____

20. Scald   _____
    Vase   _____

21. Confidence   _____
    Oxidation   _____

22. Dirt free   _____
    Thin   _____

23. Prudish; proper
    Edge
    _____
    _____

24. Try; taste
    Sufficient
    _____
    _____

25. Ship's mast
    Equal
    _____
    _____

26. Decorative plant
    Degrade; lessen
    _____
    _____

27. Prickle; spine
    Musical instrument
    _____
    _____

28. Frighten
    Supervision
    _____
    _____

29. Glimmered
    Sharpen
    _____
    _____

30. Cost
    Food staple
    _____
    _____

31. Belief
    Wing
    _____
    _____

32. Squeeze; twist
    Peal
    _____
    _____

33. Penned
    Mechanical repetition
    _____
    _____

34. Fad
    Demolish
    _____
    _____

35. Stop
    Relaxation; comfort
    _____
    _____

X Marks the Spot

Each of the 20 definitions below should lead you to a term which ends in the letter X. For example, *to churn or combine* would be MIX. How many can you supply?

10 is good; 14 is excellent; 18 means you can sit back and relax.

1. Windy City baseball team _____
2. Capital of Nova Scotia _____
3. Father of Communism _____
4. Bone in the lower spine _____
5. World-famous statue near the pyramids _____
6. Innate contradiction _____
7. Disease afflicting sheep and cattle _____
8. Capital of Arizona; mythical bird _____
9. Virginia site of Civil War surrender _____
10. American actor (*Lifeboat*, TV's *Life of Riley*) _____
11. Largest and fiercest of the dinosaurs _____
12. Suitors, boyfriends _____
13. Voice box _____
14. Segregationist former Georgia governor _____
15. Common childhood disease _____
16. Jinx; bad luck _____
17. 60's detective series starring Mike Connors _____
18. Bulging, curving outward _____
19. Southern French Atlantic port; wine from that area _____
20. Rules of grammar _____

Find the Author

On the left is a list of 13 apocryphal titles, on the right a list of their 13 putative authors. The name of each author has some affinity to one of the titles. Can you properly match up title and author?

You will find these answers a bit farfetched. All of them require some imagination, and many of them depend upon proper elision. If they were all straightforward, there would be no challenge and the whole shebang would be quite dreary. So let your mind go to lengths.

A score of 6 is run-of-the-mill; a score of 8 is good; 10 is obviously better; and a score of 12 proclaims that you're very clever. A perfect score, of course, is to be achieved only by a linguist.

TITLES

1. *Parachute Jumping*
2. *The Inevitable Occurrence*
3. *Run for Your Lives*
4. *Blowing the Big One*
5. *No Matter What*
6. *R.S.V.P.*
7. *Bar Kochba's Rebellion*
8. *The Empty Glass*
9. *Pulling Teeth*
10. *Tiger on the Prowl*
11. *Valedictorian*
12. *Hope for the Future*
13. *Written Statements*

AUTHORS

Phillipa Karef

Claude Foote

Prosper T. Combs

Helen Hiwadder

Sue Nora Lador

Willie Maykit

R. Hugh Cumming

Thomasina Tournament

C. Myra Port

Judy Fiant

Rufus Caving

Lord Howard Hertz

Hedda DeClasse

Mr. Farmer's Farm

Mr. Farmer is a farmer, and on his farm he has four hired hands: a carter, a driver, a ploughman, and a shepherd. Their names, coincidentally enough, are Mr. Carter, Mr. Driver, Mr. Ploughman, and Mr. Shepherd. It wold be very convenient if each of them had the name corresponding to his job, but unfortunately none of them has.

The problem doesn't end there. Each of the four gentlemen has a son who assists one of the others (that is, none of them assists his own father). Nor is any of the sons apprenticed to the hired hand whose vocation is the son's name.

With the following clues, can you fill in the table to show who does what?

1. Mr. Ploughman's son is engaged to the sister of the carter's apprentice.

2. The carter is married to Mr. Ploughman's sister.

3. Mr. Shepherd is married to the ploughman's widowed mother.

4. Mr. Driver's son is his only child.

TIME: 20 MINUTES

Mr. Carter	_____	Mr. Ploughman	_____
Mr. Carter's son	_____	Mr. Ploughman's son	_____
Mr. Driver	_____	Mr. Shepherd	_____
Mr. Driver's son	_____	Mr. Shepherd's son	_____

The Blind Man Sees

Three men are seated around a circular table facing each other. They are told that a box in the room contains five hats—three white and two black. A hat is placed on each man's head. Two hats remain in the box. No man sees the hat that is placed on his own head.

One man is then asked what color hat he believes to be on his head. He looks at the two hats on the heads of his companions, and then says he doesn't know.

The second man in reply to the same question admits that he too, doesn't really know.

The question is then put to the third man, *who is blind*. He correctly announces the color of the hat on his head.

Can you tell what color that hat was, and can you outline the reasoning which the blind man followed?

The Counterfeit Coin

A king of ancient days once wished to reward one of his wise men. He had his servants lay before the sage nine coins and a balance scale.

Addressing the object of his largesse, the king said, "There are nine coins here. Eight of them are made of pure gold. One of them has been debased by a lesser metal which, of course, does not weigh as much as gold.

"Now," continued the king, "you will determine your own reward. If you weigh each coin separately, you will, of course, find out which coin weighs the least, and that one will obviously be the counterfeit coin. But if you proceed in that manner, you will be obliged to use the balance scale nine times. You would then achieve the worst result, for every time you use the scale, you lose one coin. You can take 15 minutes to think about how best to proceed. Since you are a very wise man, you will manage to use the balance scale the fewest possible times and gain the highest reward."

The sage retired for a few minutes, and then came back and addressed himself to the king. "Sire," he said, "I am now ready to pick the counterfeit coin." And he proceeded to do this using the scale the least number of times necessary to determine which of the nine coins was the counterfeit.

HOW MANY TIMES DID HE USE THE SCALE?
HOW DID HE CONTRIVE TO FIND OUT?

Truth in Labeling

On a shelf in Ann's pantry are five home-canned jars. Her neighbors gave them to her at various times and she is very happy to have them. She carefully wrote on each jar what it contained, who gave it to her, and when. But her son tore off the labels. Using the 15 clues below, can you help Ann sort out the information and relabel the jars correctly?

1. Pat gave the corn.
2. The tomato juice is between two other jars.
3. The green beans were canned in 1974.
4. The sweet pickles are in the first jar.
5. The grape juice is next to the tomato juice.
6. Carol gave the fifth jar.
7. Maggie gave the jar canned in 1973.
8. Kris gave the middle jar.
9. The 1972 jar is neither on an end nor in the center.
10. The oldest jar was packed in 1969.
11. Lois gave one of the end jars.
12. The tomato juice was packed in 1973.
13. The second jar has corn in it.
14. The green beans are between two other jars.
15. 1971 was a good year for grape juice.

Typing Trouble

Steve has a very special typewriter. Each key has three things on it: a combination of two capital letters, a one- or two-digit number, and a symbol. Trouble is, Steve can't seem to memorize which go with which. Using the 11 clues given below, you should be able to figure out which letters, numbers and symbol are combined on each key and help Steve learn them. The sign = means "goes with," and the sign ≠ means "does not go with."

1. 77 = BC

2. DF = @

3. 5 ≠ % or *

4. JK = &

5. 94 ≠ GH

6. NP = 26

7. 92 ≠ LM

8. 36 = $

9. 26 ≠ #

10. LM = *

11. & ≠ 92

The Right Type

Maria has a very special typewriter. It has just five keys, which together give her 20 different typing possibilities. Each key contains a pair of capital letters, a pair of lower case letters, a two-digit number and a symbol. Maria has a very complicated system for remembering which four things go together on each key. But you can figure out your own system. Using the 14 clues given below you should be able to reconstruct Maria's typewriter keyboard. Remember that = means "goes with," and ≠ means "does not go with."

1.	PT = ou	
2.	eu ≠ 23	
3.	LM = #	
4.	70 = ¢	
5.	ao = DF	
6.	$ = 23	
7.	35 = eu	

8.	ae = 68	
9.	16 = %	
10.	* = ZQ	
11.	ie = $	
12.	XY = 23	
13.	35 ≠ #	
14.	¢ ≠ ao	

Melting Pot

America has been called the melting pot of the world because people come from many other countries to settle here. Five men came to the United States from five different countries, and their passports got mixed up in immigration.

Using the nine clues given below, you should be able to figure out the nationality of each man and return the passports to their rightful owners. You should also know the occupation of each man.

1. Pete is from Greece.
2. Ed is not from Norway.
3. The carpenter is from Italy.
4. Paul is not the doctor.
5. The Englishman is a tailor.
6. Chris is not from Iceland.
7. Andy is a teacher.
8. Chris is an engineer.
9. Paul is from England.

Campus Fun

Peter has to choose among the four colleges in his state. He knows that each school has a team with its own distinctive colors that excels in one particular sport. But he seems to get them mixed up. Using the nine clues given below you should be able to straighten Peter out. Can you identify for each college the name of its team, its color, and the sport it excels in?

1. State University wears blue and white.
2. The Bulls play for Compass College.
3. The Bears' best sport is baseball.
4. United American University wears yellow and blue.
5. The Bobcats always win at football.
6. Central State College has the best track team.
7. The Bears are from United American University.

8. The Canaries wear yellow and brown.
9. The best swimming team wears tan and green.

Match Them Up

Six Senators and their wives are having a barbeque. The men are discussing the bills they wish to introduce before the Senate. You are eavesdropping and you pick up the information contained in the 14 clues below. Can you then figure out the name of each Senator's wife and the state each couple comes from? Also identify what bill each Senator is sponsoring.

1. Peggy married the Senator from Utah.
2. Senator Clawson is sponsoring a bill on military athletics.
3. Jane did not marry the Senator from Indiana.
4. The state of Ohio elected Jim Jones as a Senator.
5. The Senator from Maine is sponsoring a bill on the National Leaf.
6. Employment for the handicapped is being sponsored by Senator Henry.
7. Senator Johnson does not represent any state West of Ohio.
8. Senator and Mrs. Jill Clawson come from Sun City, Idaho.
9. Senator Henry is from Georgia.
10. The Indiana Senator wants to make St. Patrick's Day a national holiday.
11. Senator Rooney's wife is named Corrine.
12. Mary's husband is sponsoring a bill about school busing.
13. Senator Smith is sponsoring a bill on a federal library.
14. Kathy did not marry a southern senator.

The Five Office Boys

Five office boys were examined by their employer in reading, writing, arithmetic, geography and history. A total of ten points was awarded in each subject; the boys were ranked so that each boy received 0, 1, 2, 3 or 4 points in each subject.

Each scored 4 points in one of the test areas, and the ranking for the whole examination was: first place, Les; second place, Oscar; third place, George; fourth place, Ira; and fifth place, Chuck. Given the following clues, can you fill in the table below with each boy's score in each subject and his total score?

PAR TIME: 27 minutes

	Reading	Writing	Arithmetic	Geography	History	Total
Les						
Oscar						
George						
Ira						
Chuck						

A. Chuck was tops in history, and Oscar was tops in geography.

B. George was tops in reading. He received the same number of points in writing as in arithmetic, and the same in geography as in history. He didn't get any zeros.

C. Ira was tops in writing and third in arithmetic.

D. In reading, Chuck was second and Les was third.

E. Oscar was not bottom in anything. In two subjects he did better than Les.

F. Chuck scored as many points in one subject as he did in the other four put together.

G. Les was second in both writing and geography.

Military Secrets

Four servicemen—Bob, Sam, Ken and Tom—met at the USO. They were from different home states and four different branches of the Armed Services, and no two had the same hobby. Given the clues below, can you fill in the grid so that each soldier is matched with his state, service, and hobby?

PAR TIME: 10 minutes

	Bob	Sam	Tom	Ken
State				
Hobby				
Service				

1. Ken is a Navy man.
2. The Army man likes to dance.
3. Tom likes to play baseball.
4. Sam is from Kansas.
5. The Army man is not from Kansas.
6. Someone collects stamps, but it's not the Marine.
7. Tom is not the Ohioan.
8. The Air Force man does not play cards, but one of the others does.
9. Bob is from Utah.
10. The Marine is from Maine.

The Blind Abbot

An old medieval tale tells of a blind abbot who had 20 prodigal monks under his care. He and his charges lived in the top story of a square tower which was arranged in nine cells. He himself occupied the center cell.

Each night it was his habit to patrol the abbey and to count his charges in order to make sure that the monks were all at home. His own peculiar method of tallying was to count nine heads for each wall. If he got a full count, he took it for granted that all were present.

Now a certain sly fellow arranged the beds in each cell so that two of the boys could leave of a night and make whoopee without the old codger suspecting anyone of A.W.O.L.

On another night, this shrewd young fellow even contrived to bring in four comrades from a neighboring monastery for a party. He arranged the group so cleverly that when the abbot made his evening round, he still counted only nine heads along each wall.

A few months later, the boys decided to give a grand blow-out. They increased the total attendance to 32, but still the abbot did not sense that anything was amiss.

And as a grand finale, they held one big gala super-affair; 36 monks stayed in the tower, but still the blind abbot counted but nine heads along each wall.

Now your problem is to discover how that wily brother arranged the monks in each cell so that 18, 20, 24, 32, and 36 friars were present, although in each case the blind abbot counted nine heads along each wall of the tower.

Papa's Plants

Everyone in our family has a hobby—Papa raises plants. In our house each room has one window, and each window faces a different direction. Papa has a different plant in each window, and each plant has a different color pot. Of course Papa knows exactly which pot each plant is in, and which direction each plant faces; but the rest of the family keeps forgetting. Using the 11 clues below, can you figure out which room each plant is in; the color of the pot each plant is in; and the direction each plant faces?

1. The African violet has a north window.
2. The yellow pot does not have a west window.
3. The red pot is in the playroom.
4. The blue pot is not in the living room.
5. The philodendron is in the den.
6. The coleus is not in the playroom.
7. The kitchen has a south window.
8. The spider plant is not in the living room.
9. The green pot faces south.
10. The spider plant has an east view.
11. The coleus is in the green pot.

The Adventurous Snail

Two philosophers were walking in a garden when one of them noticed a snail making the perilous ascent of a wall 20 feet high. Judging by the trail, the gentlemen calculated that the snail ascended three feet each day, sleeping and slipping back two feet each night.

"Pray tell me," said one philosopher to his companion, "how long will it take the snail to climb to the top of the wall and descend the other side. The top of the wall, as you know, has a sharp edge, so that when he gets there he will instantly begin to descend, putting precisely the same exertion into his daily climbing down as he did in his climbing up, and sleeping and slipping at night as before."

CAN YOU FIGURE OUT THE ANSWER?
(ASSUME THAT THE DAY IS EQUALLY DIVIDED INTO 12 HOURS
OF DAYTIME CLIMBING AND 12 HOURS OF SLEEPING AT NIGHT.)

Typesetter's Headache

Roger is learning to operate a computer typewriter. He started on this simple machine which has only four keys. However, each key has a combination of two letters, a symbol, and a number. Roger is having trouble remembering which letters go with which symbols and numbers. From the 7 clues below you should be able to straighten him out. Remember, = means "goes with"; ≠ means "does not go with."

1. XY = 57

2. TR = $

3. LK = %

4. 68 ≠ ES

5. 101 = @

6. 39 ≠ #

7. LK ≠ 39

Typesetter's Nightmare

Roger has graduated to a slightly more complicated machine. On this one there are five keys, each one with a two-letter consonant combination. Each of these keys goes with its own two-digit number, its own symbol, and its own lower case vowel. Using the 13 clues given below, help Roger sort out the consonants, number, symbol, and vowel that go together on each key. Remember, = means "go together," and ≠ means "does not go together."

1. ST = 56

2. 28 ≠ FG

3. 13 = !

4. ZX = 79

5. FG = i

6. u = 13

7. # = e

8. 98 ≠ *

9. MN = o

10. a = %

11. LK = u

12. & ≠ MN

13. a ≠ ZX

The Lonesome Prairie

Six lonesome cowboys are sitting around the campfire discussing the thing that all cowboys talk about: their horses. They are from six different states. In the light of the campfire can be seen their cowboy hats—in six different colors. With the 15 clues below, can you assign a home state, a hat, and a horse, of course, to each lonesome cowboy?

TIME: 10 MINUTES

	Barney	Cal	Chuck	Del	Slim	Al
HORSE'S NAME						
HAT COLOR						
HOME STATE						

1. Patches is Chuck's horse.

2. The blue hat belongs to Blue's rider.

3. Al wears a yellow hat.

4. Cal wears neither the red hat nor the blue one.

5. Cal comes from Utah.

6. Del rides Blaze.

7. Slim rides Berry, not Blue.

8. Al is not the Texan.

9. Wyoming is Barney's home state.

10. Ringo carries the cowboy from Nevada.

11. The cowboy who wears a brown hat comes from Colorado.

12. Slim was born in Oklahoma.

13. Red River and the green hat belong to the same cowboy.

14. Chuck wears the red Stetson.

15. The tan hat belongs to the Oklahoman.

64

The Soccer Tournament

Four high schools—Central, Madison, Lakeside and Western—competed in an all-city soccer tournament. Each school played each of the others once. In each game, two points were at stake: the winner received two points, but if the two teams tied, each received one point.

At the end of the tournament, the total was: Madison, 5 points; Central 3 points; Western, 3 points; Lakeside, 1 point.

In the entire tournament, a total of thirteen goals was scored, seven of them by Central High alone; Western High scored no goals at all.

In the game between Central and Lakeside, Central won four goals to one.

Can you fill in the scores to the other five games?

TIME: 12 MINUTES

Central-Madison	_____
Central-Lakeside	____4–1____
Central-Western	_____
Madison-Lakeside	_____
Madison-Western	_____
Lakeside-Western	_____

65

Variety Is the Spice

Four high school teachers met at a national convention in New York City. They are from three different states, and they teach four different subjects. They are having a hard time deciding where to go out for dinner in the big city because they have four different preferences in ethnic foods. From the clues given, can you fill in the grid to show who teaches what, who eats what, and who is from what state?

TIME: FIVE MINUTES

	Dorothy	George	Earl	Walt
CUISINE				
SUBJECT				
STATE				

1. Dorothy and George are from the same state.

2. Texas is the home of the French teacher.

3. The English teacher is not the one who likes Chinese food.

4. Earl teaches geography.

5. The math teacher loves Mexican food.

6. The Texan hates French food.

7. The English teacher comes from Indiana.

8. Dorothy is not the one who loves Italian food.

9. The French-food fan is from Oregon.

10. George teaches English.

Sugar and Spice

It is Friday night after the big game. Six cheerleaders from Naughton High School are having a slumber party. Besides their boyfriends (of course), the girls talk about their favorite TV shows. No two of them have the same favorite program, and, luckily, no two of them have the same boyfriend. The girls are sleeping in sleeping bags of six different colors. Given the clues below, can you indicate in the grid which girl has which boyfriend; which girl has which sleeping bag; and which girl watches what TV show?

TIME: SEVEN MINUTES

	Lois	Mary	Margie	Shirley	Diane	Sharon
BAG						
BOYFRIEND						
TV SHOW						

1. Lois dates Scott and watches *M*A*S*H*.
2. Ken's girlfriend brought a plaid sleeping bag.
3. Mary brought a blue sleeping bag.
4. Margie dates Andy.
5. Sharon never misses *American Bandstand*, but someone else prefers *Maude*.
6. The owner of the green sleeping bag dates Ed.
7. Shirley likes *Laverne and Shirley*.
8. Diane's favorite show is not *Hawaii Five-O*, but it is someone else's favorite.
9. Margie did not bring the red sleeping bag.
10. Ben's date watches *Happy Days* faithfully.
11. Sharon brought the plaid bag, not the yellow one.
12. Diane dates Al and brought a black sleeping bag.

67

Middle Diddle

It's quite a fiddle to muddle to the middle, especially with those arrows blocking your path. Move from the top to the "X" in the center. Go only in the direction the arrow is pointing. Time yourself. Twelve minutes is middling; 9 minutes is obviously better; and 6 minutes or less is a real accomplishment.

69

Bouquet

Like a drop of rain, enter on top through the flower and go down to the roots. Time yourself. If you can find the route in 15 minutes, you've got nothing to be ashamed of; 12 minutes is good; 10 minutes or less and you come up roses.

Anamaze

Start with the letter "T" in the heavy-bordered box just below and left of center, and travel only from box to adjoining box to form words. There's a 7-word sentence hidden in this maze, beginning with "The" and ending with a punctuation mark.

A solution in less than 10 minutes is unusual.

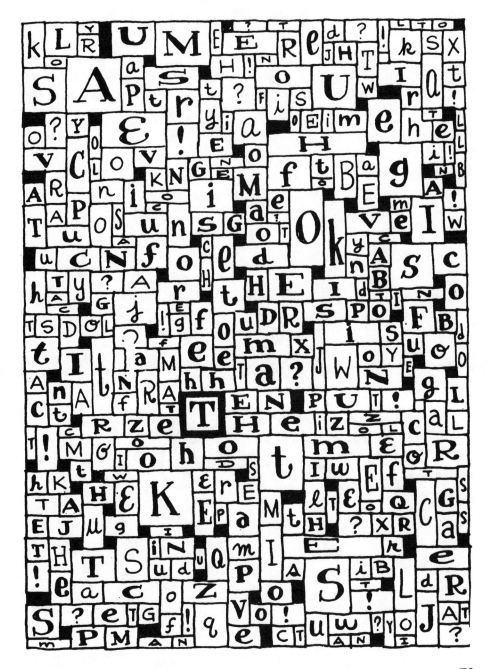

73

Spaghetti

Here's a twist: a three-dimensional maze. You can go over or under, but you must pass the arrows in the right direction. Working your way from top to bottom, 7 minutes is just dandy; and 5 minutes or less makes you the fastest spaghetti eater in town.

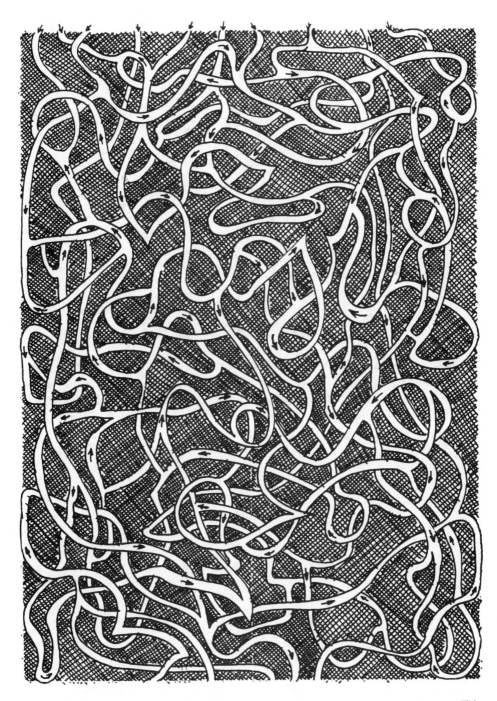

75

Square or Circle

Choose either the square or circle and follow it through to the end. You may only pass through an oval that contains your pick, and you may only travel in the same direction as the arrow along your path. Whichever shape you choose, your voyage shouldn't take more than 5 minutes, and if it's done in 3 minutes or less, you're too good for this maze!

Pick Up Sticks

A game that's been around for a long time is called "Pick Up Sticks." Here are the sticks, all piled on top of one another. This one's tough, but stick it out. A solution in 16 minutes is not bad; 13 minutes, very good; and 10 minutes or less—well, you *are* good!

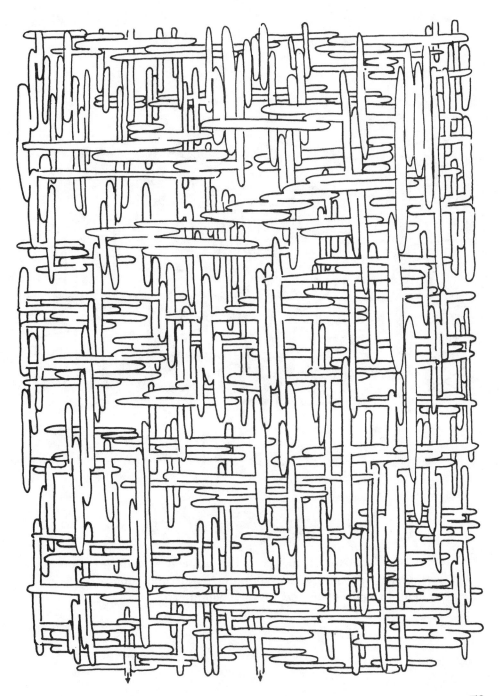

On the Square

A square is two-dimensional, and so is this maze: you can't go under another passageway. A solution in 7 minutes is fair and square; in 5 minutes, excellent; in 3 minutes or less, simply magnificent!

Half and Half

Start at the top; exit at the bottom; but *you must enter each half of the maze at least once, traveling only in the direction of the arrows.* In the right half, you may proceed through the "underpasses" when the paths cross.

   If you can wend your way through in 12 minutes, that's nothing to brag about; 10 minutes is decent; and 7 minutes or less shows you're very quick indeed.

83

Map Problem

Three highways enter this maze at the top, but only one exits at the bottom. There are overpasses and underpasses, and some streets are one-way. A trip completed in 10 minutes is slow but sure; 8 minutes, a bit better; and 6 minutes or less—slow down, you're speeding!

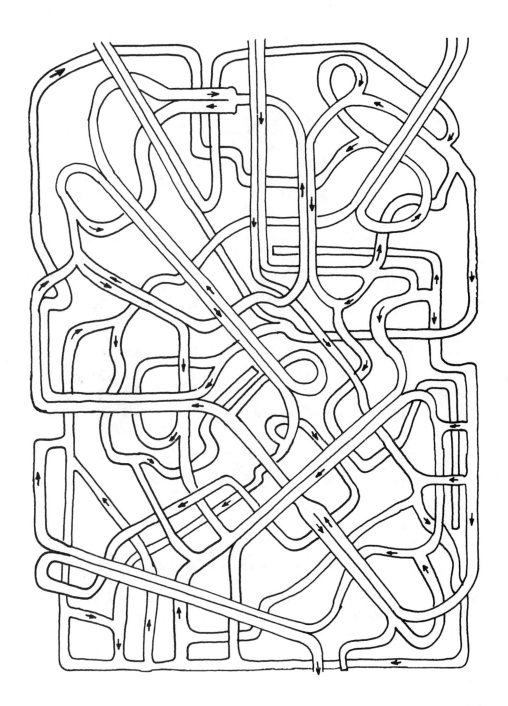

85

Collywobbles

Some say you get the collywobbles, some say the collywobbles get you. Anyway, get through this one in 8 minutes for a passing grade; 6 minutes for an excellent score; and 4 minutes or less for a mark of distinction.

How to Solve Blankies

The *Blankie* is based on progressive anagrams. Each Blankie is a short story in itself. In each story, a number of words have been omitted. Each omitted word is indicated by a number of dashes. Each dash represents a single letter. For example, a series of three dashes indicates a three-letter word; a series of four dashes, a four-letter word, etc.

The key word in the Blankie is set down in capital letters. Every successive word must include the letters contained in the previous word, plus one additional letter.

For example, with the key word AT, the successive words might be AT, CAT, TACK, STACK, TRACKS. Inferences drawn from the content should be of great help in suggesting the missing words.

Guilty but Whitewashed

Now I've had cats and I've had dogs, and I've had birds, and I've had reptiles, but my little terrier Cutie is the sweetest, dearest, darlingest *P E T* I've ever had. She's so nervy, fresh, vivacious, and _ _ _ _ _, and particularly so when she does something wrong. I certainly give her enough to eat. She gets all kinds of meat, especially _ _ _ _ _ _.

But she's a born _ _ _ _ _ _ _. She steals. It isn't that she's hungry. It's just that she loves to filch things. When we have _ _ _ _ _ _ _ _ at our house and have prepared platters of cakes and eclairs, she invades the kitchen and when no one is looking, grabs off a few delectable creampuffs. And then, right before every one else, as if she were innocent as a goldfish, she _ _ _ _ _ _ _ _ _ into the parlor before all the guests, with her face full of whipped cream.

She's small; she's weak; she's no good as a watchdog; the plain fact is she's useless, but one of the most delightful _ _ _ _ _ _ _ _ _ _ alive.

Ah! The French!

The Countess was charming, the Countess was beautiful. The Countess was vain, the Countess was fickle. But the Countess had the most graceful figure in Paris, and the Countess had passionate eyes. When he came along, the Countess had countless suitors. But he discounted them in advance. Soon, his rival, the Count de Rose, was accounted as nothing, and Viscount Bretonne was accounted as twice nothing, and her resistance was *N I L* . She swallowed his American _ _ _ _, with hook and sinker.

He pleaded that she become his immediately. She countered with two weeks. He counted the days. As soon as they were married, they took an ocean _ _ _ _ _ for the States. Now that he had won his prize, why _ _ _ _ _ _ _ in Europe? He had been warned of her capriciousness, but he took no account of these scandalous rumors.

The third day out he became quite dizzy. He took a drink to counteract his seasickness, but this only made it worse. His brain was _ _ _ _ _ _ _. Stumbling below deck, he managed to reach their stateroom, and burst in without knocking.

There stood the Countess. Evidently she had not counted on his coming at that hour. She blushed! She couldn't speak. He was bewildered! He couldn't speak. What an encounter!

Yes, there stood the Countess, at high noon, quite nude, fondling her _ _ _ _ _ _ _ _ _. Ah! The French! The French!

Love, Love, Love

When it comes to love, there *A R E* girls who _ _ _ _, girls who _ _ _ _ _ _, and girls who _ _ _ _ _ _ _.

Mine _ _ _ _ _ _ _ _! It's delightful!   But it sounds like a _ _ _ _ _ _ _ _!

The Song We Thrill To

The finest tonic for jagged nerves, the sweetest music to the *E A R* is disguised flattery. One word carefully sown can _ _ _ _ a harvest of friendship. Like a _ _ _ _ _ well-directed, honeyed words pierce the heart.

There is only one man I ever knew who didn't either inwardly or outwardly enjoy _ _ _ _ _ _. He had _ _ _ _ _ _ _.

Defenders of the Faith

There is nothing that arouses my *I R E* so much as the arrogant and presumptuous remark, calculated to vex and _ _ _ _ social reformers of foreign extraction, that declares, "If you don't like this country, why don't you go back where you came from."

This particular brand of heckling should really heat the _ _ _ _ _ of any true American, for such _ _ _ _ _ _ specifically ignores and undermines American traditions. The remark implies that foreign-born citizens have not the same prerogatives as natural-born citizens. By such doctrine is the Constitution, which provides freedom of speech, slandered and _ _ _ _ _ _.

Pseudo-patriots seem to think that they are often dispensationally _ _ _ _ _ _ _ _ from according equal rights of expression to naturalized foreign-born citizens. Our country need fear nothing from peaceful speech, no matter how clamorous or bitter, but it may well be _ _ _ _ _ _ _ _ _ from the sedition of those false Americans who would throttle every idea that is not their own.

90   (DIRECTIONS FOR SOLVING BLANKIES ARE ON PAGE 88)

The Haunted House

Frank and Sam had thought about the possibilites of that haunted house for a long time. Finally they laid plans *T O* pull the town up by the ears.

One misty night, Frank __ __ __ into some old __ __ __ __ and Sam draped him in a white sheet. Then, Sam spread the word that the haunted house was again the habitation of a shade.

A few lads, stung by Sam's dares, advanced in a group upon the creaky cabin, but only Frank's sepulchral wail was needed to rout them. A crowd soon gathered, standing off at a safe distance. It heard hardy men boast of their fearlessness. And it saw each one of these same men, in turn, enter the cabin and emerge the next second in full flight, pursued for a few steps by the filmy form of the __ __ __ __ __ ! Even thugs and hard-boiled __ __ __ __ __ __ quailed before the spectral terror.

Then, when all the town's he-men had been turned to milk, Sam saw a queer thing happen. Suddenly the tables were turned! There was Frank, screaming and terrified, tearing off his shroud, running away from the cabin as if pursued by the devil.

It seems that a stranger had stalked in to meet the specter with a __ __ __ __ __ __ __ !

The Path of True Love

It is a dollar to a dime, or *T E N* to one, that when emotions are __ __ __ __ up, girls become befuddled and manually __ __ __ __ __ __ .

When grappling with a girdle, many a hot mama has wished, "Ah! if this were only a __ __ __ __ __ __ or __ __ __ __ __ __ __ !

(DIRECTIONS FOR SOLVING BLANKIES ARE ON PAGE 88)

Blankies in Verse I

Blankies in Verse is a word game based on anagrams, such as TEAM, MATE, MEAT. Each Blankie is a short poem in itself. In each poem a number of words have been omitted, indicated by dashes. Each dash represents a single letter. The missing words in any one poem all contain the same letters arranged in a different order. Look for a clue within the poem to help you get started.

1. The typist and _ _ _ _ _ was good at his work

    Till a _ _ _ _ _ with bullets was aimed at this clerk.

    The killer, a _ _ _ _ _ who just went berserk

    Is a _ _ _ _ _ in jail now, the poor little jerk.

2. The _ _ _ _ _ _ _ flicks his tongue with malice

    While all those _ _ _ _ _ _ _ drink from the chalice.

    Not one _ _ _ _ _ _ _ this terrible sin,

    Nor sees the creature slithering in.

3. The red-head who came from the _ _ _ _ _ _ state

    _ _ _ _ _ _ into the party some two hours late,

    Well _ _ _ _ _ _ in her jeans and quite drunk from some beer.

    "Oh, you're in the _ _ _, _ _ _," someone hissed in her ear. (*2 wds.*)

4. The King was so _ _ _ _ _ and so wicked and old;

    He drank all his _ _ _ _ _ _ from mugs of pure gold.

    With his haughty _ _ _ _ _ _ he was as sharp as an eagle;

    His courtiers feared this fat ruler so _ _ _ _ _.

(DIRECTIONS FOR SOLVING BLANKIES ARE ON PAGE 88)

5. _ _ _ _ _ _ Dame was the name of a lovely French goose

Who _ _ _ _ _ _ in her _ _ _ _ _ _ so free and so loose.

Through fences of wire a _ _ _ _ _ _ she spied;

Ignoring the _ _ _ _ _ _ she flew to his side.

6. The man in the diner was definitely crude,

His nails down to the _ _ _ _ he chewed.

He'd _ _ _ _ the waitress, and what a deal!

He'd eat the _ _ _ _, but order no meal.

7. The lady dons her _ _ _ _ at night,

And buckled _ _ _ _ that fits just right.

But all day long, she's in the yard,

With rakes and _ _ _ _ she's working hard.

8. The _ _ _ _ _ took off his big white hat,

"I need a _ _ _ _ _ and that is that."

He drove his car to a house in the valley,

Put on his _ _ _ _ _ and parked in the alley.

9. The old Latin scholar, _ _ _ _ _ _ and enthralled,

Looked up where a _ _ _ _ _ _ of Caesar was installed.

The crowd roared with laughter at this poor bloke,

_ _ "_ _ _ _, Brute" were the words that he spoke.

(DIRECTIONS FOR SOLVING BLANKIES ARE ON PAGE 88)   93

A Business Conference

Mae's *I R E* was up, but her boss remained calm. "Mae," he said, interrupting her latest tirade, "you _ _ _ _ me with your ridiculous accusations."

"Don't play dumb with me," she shouted. "Every time I come in here to take dictation you sit there and _ _ _ _ _ your eyes on my legs. I just want you to understand one thing. I'm a woman of _ _ _ _ _ _ _."

"You mean I'm not supposed to even look at you?"

"Well," she hedged, "you could at least be more _ _ _ _ _ _ _ about it."

Answers on page 117

Payment Deferred

"Yes, this *I S* 39 Marly Street, all right. Tim Healy? Yes, but he's not at home. I'm a friend of _ _ _. You want to collect _ _ _ _ bill? Can't blame you for that. Well, you're going to have tough going, brother. He's broke, stone broke. Yes, he did work last week. Right again, he did make $50. But he went and got himself pickled and then got into a poker game and lost his _ _ _ _ _.

"Say, how's he going to raise $35? He's got no credit. He can't raise a dime. The only thing he can raise is a _ _ _ _ _ _."

After the Dance Marathon

"Hello, Myrtle, how are you?"

"O.K., *P A*."

"Worn out, I suppose. How's your friend, Joe?"

"Friend? He's no _ _ _ of mine any more. Why I'd like to brain him!"

(DIRECTIONS FOR SOLVING BLANKIES ARE ON PAGE 88)

"Now, Myrtle, don't get yourself excited. You look bad enough as it is. You're as _ _ _ _ as a ghost."

"Well, what do you expect after four days of steady dancing?"

"I told you not to get into that crazy...."

"All right, Pa. It's all over now. I had my lesson. Ow! How my feet ache! That guy Joe! Why at least I should have come home with a thousand dollars in cash for all this. That $2,000 prize was in the bag, Pa! In the bag!

"By yesterday, there were only three couples left. This morning one of 'em drops out, and the other couple starts in to stagger. In a few hours, they need smellin' salts to keep them going.

"By then I'm so drowsy I feel as if I'm in a coma. But Joe, he's spry and chipper and _ _ _ _ _ around like a gazelle. All he keeps saying is 'Hold out, kid, we're practically home.' Easy to say, with me half dead and him as fresh as a daisy!"

"Then, as the judges decide to eliminate that other couple for stalling, and the attendant is sent to escort them off the floor, Pa, whaddya think that big-shot guy Joe does? With the first prize practically in our hands, he falls dead _ _ _ _ _ _ _!"

(DIRECTIONS FOR SOLVING BLANKIES ARE ON PAGE 88)

Righteous Indignation

There *A R E* certain base journals which lust to report a _ _ _ _ and take no pains to _ _ _ _ _ the details.

Could any decent person help but despise such venality? No! Assuredly no!

Could any decent person ever enjoy reading such _ _ _ _ _ _? All Nature, all the world, every college conclave, every educational conference, every group of men and women of wisdom, rise and answer "_ _ _ _ _ _ _."

Introductory

There has descended upon *A N* avid public an avalanche of word games. The crossword puzzle has made many a torpid brain cell busy as an _ _ _ _. Though the circumspect _ _ _ _ _ that such mental exercises are more work than relaxation, the puzzler himself, lost in an absorbing _ _ _ _ _ of thought, seems blissfully oblivious of everything except his eventual _ _ _ _ _ _.

Some of these Blankies are as hard as _ _ _ _ _ _ _ _. But they can all be solved by the patient application of logic. Analysis of the sense of the paragraph as a whole is a prerequisite to the solution. It is all a matter of arranging the _ _ _ _ _ _ _ _ _ letters in proper sequence so that the correct word is formed. The correct word is invariably the logical word.

Courage above all! Though you may find that your first efforts are weak and _ _ _ _ _ _ _ _ _, be assured that ultimate success will prove extremely _ _ _ _ _ _ _ _ _ _ to the ego.

(DIRECTIONS FOR SOLVING BLANKIES ARE ON PAGE 88)

Postscript

Do the Blankies which follow vary in difficulty? The answer is *Y E S*. This one, for example, is very __ __ __ __. Other solutions might take from five to twenty minutes, perhaps a couple of hours, now and then a week, or even a month, and for some people __ __ __ __ __.

Usually one letter is added at a time. But, occasionally, as in the next word to be supplied, two letters must be added. The best thing to do in a case like this is to sharpen your pencil, sharpen your wits, drop to your knees and say your __ __ __ __ __ __ __.

Come into My Parlor

They walked *I N* to her apartment, crazily, with mock solemnity, saturated with __ __ __. She stood quite still as he, like elf, sprite, or evil __ __ __ __ __*, hovered about her. She seemed hypnotized while he, with demoniacal calm, divested her naiad form of its silken raiment. Soon she stood quite nude.

Then he began __ __ __ __ __ __ her meticulously, but his gaze was not that of the rapt connoisseur of beauty. Lust lurked in his eye, and the tranquil certitude of his movements embarrassed her.

"What are you doing?" she cried. "Why are you staring at me so?"

Then a picaresque gleam appeared in his eye as he said carelessly, "Oh, just a mere matter of __ __ __ __ __ __ __, my dear."

*This word has two more letters than the previous word.

Undercover Business

"N O, Mr. Smithers, it's __ __ __ that I haven't got the money; it's just that the __ __ __ __ of this piano is simply awful! How do I know? Why you'd have to be __ __ __ __ __ deaf not to hear just how false the notes are!

"Do I take care of it? Say, Mr. Smithers, whom do you think you're talking to? Yes, I know it's a baby grand! I know the cover has to be lifted and the hammers dusted. Why, I've dusted those hammers every day! And your firm is supposed to be __ __ __ __ __ __, cheating me with that cheap instrument."

All unperturbed, Mr. Smithers walked over to the piano and began to lift the cover. Madam was close at his heels. Immediately he raised the sounding board, a whirring noise was heard. Suddenly a mass of black jumped out at the lady! She recoiled screaming!

* * *

"Did you collect the due payment from Mrs. Mackintosh, Smithers?"

"Yes, sir, and more! She was that embarrassed she paid me the whole balance! When I came to the house she claimed she'd been stung. Well, she was! Inside her piano, which she claimed she cleaned every day, there were—of all things! __ __ __ __ __ __ __!"

A Slight Omission

Armand J. Hoopenpopper stepped bouyantly into the street on his way *T O* his first job. He was determined to put his flighty past behind him and _ _ _ the mark. And even though he wanted to be a _ _ _ _, he was resolved to do well in his job as a messenger.

As he walked into the office the boss said, "Hoopenpopper, I want you go to the bank next to the train _ _ _ _ _. Here's the cash; the teller will know what to do with it." He then proceeded to give him the account information.

After Hoopenpopper was sure he'd been thoroughly _ _ _ _ _ _, off he went to the bank. There the teller went over what Hoopenpopper had brought in and looked up at him. "Nicely done, Armand, but you forgot one little thing: the _ _ _ _ _ _ _."

O Tempora! O Mores!

The debt and the note were both *D U E*, and she could not discharge them by cash payment. Accordingly, she proceeded to his home, as she had promised, _ _ _ _ _, _ _ _ _ _ _ her ermine cloak.

His excitement knew no bounds. Well, her virtue and her cloak were both _ _ _ _ _ _ _. But she didn't care! The cloak was _ _ _ _ _ _ _ _!

(DIRECTIONS FOR SOLVING BLANKIES ARE ON PAGE 88)

Life's Little Jokes

When I was a lad, my greatest delight was reading stories of adventure—peril and escape. I was magnetized by books. When engrossed in a heroic yarn, neither food nor sleep could pull me away from the printed page. My mother literally had to *D R A G* me off to meals and bed.

In those golden days, I lived in a _ _ _ _ _ and glorious world of adventure. I was fascinated by tales whose chief ingredient was _ _ _ _ _ _. Consequently, I was continuously _ _ _ _ _ _ _ books like *In Darkest Africa* and similar works about exploration, jungle fights, savages, and hunting. I used to sit transfixed in reverie for hours, dreaming that some day I, too, would be _ _ _ _ _ _ _ _ the lion in his den. When I grew up, I would lead a life of peril. I would be a soldier, an explorer, a deep-sea diver, a big-game hunter; at least a policeman or fireman. My ambitions lay in virile vocations.

Ah! Youth and dreams! What a let-down! What I am doing now is certainly not what I _ _ _ _ _ _ _ _ _ for! Here I am—I, who yearned for jeopardy—bottled up in a department store, a clerk in the men's clothes section, selling _ _ _ _ _ _ _ _ _ _ _.

(DIRECTIONS FOR SOLVING BLANKIES ARE ON PAGE 88)

Blankies in Verse II

BLANKIES IN VERSE is a word game based on anagrams (e.g., TEA, ATE, EAT). Each Blankie is a short poem in itself. In each poem, some words have been omitted, indicated by dashes. Each dash represents a single letter. Using context clues, rearrange the same letters to form different words for each gap.

1. The dentist was _ _ _ _ _ as he looked at her teeth,

    Poked at her _ _ _ _ _ and picked underneath.

    "You'll need some work—three fillings, I think."

    She gulped from two _ _ _ _ _ and spat in the sink.

2. He _ _ _ _ _ _ a cabin by a lake remote,

    And studies the wildlife from his boat.

    He sits in the _ _ _ _ _ _ with an eagle eye,

    Watching ducks and _ _ _ _ _ _ fly by.

3. "I'll _ _ _ _ _ _ this ball straight over to Vance,"

    Says _ _ _ _ _ _ as he levels his foe with a glance.

    He _ _ _ _ _ _ to the baseline to _ _ _ _ _ _ the rally.

    I hope this _ _ _ _ _ _ is right up your alley!

4. His _ _ _ _ _ was winning the season's big game;

    He was surprised their rivals were acting so _ _ _ _ _.

    So he said to his _ _ _ _ _ as he got to his feet,

    "We'll make of these bozos hamburger _ _ _ _ _."

(DIRECTIONS FOR SOLVING BLANKIES ARE ON PAGE 88)

How to Solve Alfabits

The idea is to try to make as many words as you can out of the letters in the word which forms the given title. The answers are governed by the following rules:

1. Words must be at least four letters in length. Plurals of two- or three-letter words (such as CATS or OXEN) are not allowed, nor are inflected forms of two- or three-letter verbs (such as GOES, EATS, and BEEN).

2. A word can be used in either the singular or the plural, but not both unless its plural changes the stem (e.g., MICE, GEESE, FEET). However, more significant additions are welcome: the use of ABLE does not preclude (provided the letters are available) UNABLE, ENABLE, or ABILITY. Once a simple verb form is used, the addition of -(E)D, -(E)S, or -ING is not allowed: LEARN is fine, but not also LEARNS, LEARNED, or LEARNING. An adjective may be used in only one of its three degrees (DEAR, DEARER, or DEAREST).

3. Proper names and obsolete or archaic words are taboo. Reformed spellings (NITE and THRU for NIGHT and THROUGH) are out.

If you can think of 50% of the possible words in each title, you're doing well; 65%, you're doing superbly; 80% or better, our hats are off to you!

Bridge

There are at least 12 words, each of four letters or more, that can be made out of the letters in the word BRIDGE.

1. _____   5. _____   9. _____

2. _____   6. _____   10. _____

3. _____   7. _____   11. _____

4. _____   8. _____   12. _____

Punctilious

There are at least 63 words, each of four letters or more, that can be made out of the letters in the word PUNCTILIOUS.

1. _____	22. _____	43. _____
2. _____	23. _____	44. _____
3. _____	24. _____	45. _____
4. _____	25. _____	46. _____
5. _____	26. _____	47. _____
6. _____	27. _____	48. _____
7. _____	28. _____	49. _____
8. _____	29. _____	50. _____
9. _____	30. _____	51. _____
10. _____	31. _____	52. _____
11. _____	32. _____	53. _____
12. _____	33. _____	54. _____
13. _____	34. _____	55. _____
14. _____	35. _____	56. _____
15. _____	36. _____	57. _____
16. _____	37. _____	58. _____
17. _____	38. _____	59. _____
18. _____	39. _____	60. _____
19. _____	40. _____	61. _____
20. _____	41. _____	62. _____
21. _____	42. _____	63. _____

Soldiers

There are at least 35 words of four letters or more that can be made out of the letters in the word SOLDIERS.

1. _____   13. _____   24. _____
2. _____   14. _____   25. _____
3. _____   15. _____   26. _____
4. _____   16. _____   27. _____
5. _____   17. _____   28. _____
6. _____   18. _____   29. _____
7. _____   19. _____   30. _____
8. _____   20. _____   31. _____
9. _____   21. _____   32. _____
10. _____   22. _____   33. _____
11. _____   23. _____   34. _____
12. _____   35. _____

Vestibule

There are at least 45 words, each of four letters or more, that can be made out of the letters in the word VESTIBULE.

1. _____   4. _____   7. _____
2. _____   5. _____   8. _____
3. _____   6. _____   9. _____

104   (DIRECTIONS FOR SOLVING ALFABITS ARE ON PAGE 102)

10. _____ 22. _____ 34. _____
11. _____ 23. _____ 35. _____
12. _____ 24. _____ 36. _____
13. _____ 25. _____ 37. _____
14. _____ 26. _____ 38. _____
15. _____ 27. _____ 39. _____
16. _____ 28. _____ 40. _____
17. _____ 29. _____ 41. _____
18. _____ 30. _____ 42. _____
19. _____ 31. _____ 43. _____
20. _____ 32. _____ 44. _____
21. _____ 33. _____ 45. _____

Sheepishly

There are at least 24 words, each of four letters or more, that can be made out of the letters in the word SHEEPISHLY.

1. _____ 9. _____ 17. _____
2. _____ 10. _____ 18. _____
3. _____ 11. _____ 19. _____
4. _____ 12. _____ 20. _____
5. _____ 13. _____ 21. _____
6. _____ 14. _____ 22. _____
7. _____ 15. _____ 23. _____
8. _____ 16. _____ 24. _____

(DIRECTIONS FOR SOLVING ALFABITS ARE ON PAGE 102)   105

Memorabilia

There are at least 68 words that can be made out of the letters in the word MEMORABILIA.

1. _____	24. _____	46. _____
2. _____	25. _____	47. _____
3. _____	26. _____	48. _____
4. _____	27. _____	49. _____
5. _____	28. _____	50. _____
6. _____	29. _____	51. _____
7. _____	30. _____	52. _____
8. _____	31. _____	53. _____
9. _____	32. _____	54. _____
10. _____	33. _____	55. _____
11. _____	34. _____	56. _____
12. _____	35. _____	57. _____
13. _____	36. _____	58. _____
14. _____	37. _____	59. _____
15. _____	38. _____	60. _____
16. _____	39. _____	61. _____
17. _____	40. _____	62. _____
18. _____	41. _____	63. _____
19. _____	42. _____	64. _____
20. _____	43. _____	65. _____
21. _____	44. _____	66. _____
22. _____	45. _____	67. _____
23. _____		68. _____

(DIRECTIONS FOR SOLVING ALFABITS ARE ON PAGE 102)

Sycophant

There are at least 62 words that can be made out of the letters in the word SYCOPHANT.

1. _____	22. _____	42. _____
2. _____	23. _____	43. _____
3. _____	24. _____	44. _____
4. _____	25. _____	45. _____
5. _____	26. _____	46. _____
6. _____	27. _____	47. _____
7. _____	28. _____	48. _____
8. _____	29. _____	49. _____
9. _____	30. _____	50. _____
10. _____	31. _____	51. _____
11. _____	32. _____	52. _____
12. _____	33. _____	53. _____
13. _____	34. _____	54. _____
14. _____	35. _____	55. _____
15. _____	36. _____	56. _____
16. _____	37. _____	57. _____
17. _____	38. _____	58. _____
18. _____	39. _____	59. _____
19. _____	40. _____	60. _____
20. _____	41. _____	61. _____
21. _____		62. _____

Spectacle

There are at least 75 words, each of four letters or more, that can be made out of the letters in the word SPECTACLE.

1. _____	23. _____	45. _____
2. _____	24. _____	46. _____
3. _____	25. _____	47. _____
4. _____	26. _____	48. _____
5. _____	27. _____	49. _____
6. _____	28. _____	50. _____
7. _____	29. _____	51. _____
8. _____	30. _____	52. _____
9. _____	31. _____	53. _____
10. _____	32. _____	54. _____
11. _____	33. _____	55. _____
12. _____	34. _____	56. _____
13. _____	35. _____	57. _____
14. _____	36. _____	58. _____
15. _____	37. _____	59. _____
16. _____	38. _____	60. _____
17. _____	39. _____	61. _____
18. _____	40. _____	62. _____
19. _____	41. _____	63. _____
20. _____	42. _____	64. _____
21. _____	43. _____	65. _____
22. _____	44. _____	66. _____

(DIRECTIONS FOR SOLVING ALFABITS ARE ON PAGE 102)

67. _____   70. _____   73. _____
68. _____   71. _____   74. _____
69. _____   72. _____   75. _____

Spokesman

There are at least 50 words, each of four letters or more, that can be made out of the letters in the word SPOKESMAN.

1. _____   18. _____   34. _____
2. _____   19. _____   35. _____
3. _____   20. _____   36. _____
4. _____   21. _____   37. _____
5. _____   22. _____   38. _____
6. _____   23. _____   39. _____
7. _____   24. _____   40. _____
8. _____   25. _____   41. _____
9. _____   26. _____   42. _____
10. _____ 27. _____   43. _____
11. _____ 28. _____   44. _____
12. _____ 29. _____   45. _____
13. _____ 30. _____   46. _____
14. _____ 31. _____   47. _____
15. _____ 32. _____   48. _____
16. _____ 33. _____   49. _____
17. _____   50. _____

(DIRECTIONS FOR SOLVING ALFABITS ARE ON PAGE 102)

Nothingness

There are at least 60 words that can be made out of the letters in the word NOTHINGNESS.

1. _____	21. _____	41. _____
2. _____	22. _____	42. _____
3. _____	23. _____	43. _____
4. _____	24. _____	44. _____
5. _____	25. _____	45. _____
6. _____	26. _____	46. _____
7. _____	27. _____	47. _____
8. _____	28. _____	48. _____
9. _____	29. _____	49. _____
10. _____	30. _____	50. _____
11. _____	31. _____	51. _____
12. _____	32. _____	52. _____
13. _____	33. _____	53. _____
14. _____	34. _____	54. _____
15. _____	35. _____	55. _____
16. _____	36. _____	56. _____
17. _____	37. _____	57. _____
18. _____	38. _____	58. _____
19. _____	39. _____	59. _____
20. _____	40. _____	60. _____

(DIRECTIONS FOR SOLVING ALFABITS ARE ON PAGE 102)

Desperado

There are at least 65 words that can be made out of the letters in the word DESPERADO.

1. _____ 23. _____ 45. _____
2. _____ 24. _____ 46. _____
3. _____ 25. _____ 47. _____
4. _____ 26. _____ 48. _____
5. _____ 27. _____ 49. _____
6. _____ 28. _____ 50. _____
7. _____ 29. _____ 51. _____
8. _____ 30. _____ 52. _____
9. _____ 31. _____ 53. _____
10. _____ 32. _____ 54. _____
11. _____ 33. _____ 55. _____
12. _____ 34. _____ 56. _____
13. _____ 35. _____ 57. _____
14. _____ 36. _____ 58. _____
15. _____ 37. _____ 59. _____
16. _____ 38. _____ 60. _____
17. _____ 39. _____ 61. _____
18. _____ 40. _____ 62. _____
19. _____ 41. _____ 63. _____
20. _____ 42. _____ 64. _____
21. _____ 43. _____ 65. _____
22. _____ 44. _____

(DIRECTIONS FOR SOLVING ALFABITS ARE ON PAGE 102)

Triumvirate

There are at least 60 words that can be made out of the letters in the word TRIUMVIRATE.

1. _____	21. _____	41. _____
2. _____	22. _____	42. _____
3. _____	23. _____	43. _____
4. _____	24. _____	44. _____
5. _____	25. _____	45. _____
6. _____	26. _____	46. _____
7. _____	27. _____	47. _____
8. _____	28. _____	48. _____
9. _____	29. _____	49. _____
10. _____	30. _____	50. _____
11. _____	31. _____	51. _____
12. _____	32. _____	52. _____
13. _____	33. _____	53. _____
14. _____	34. _____	54. _____
15. _____	35. _____	55. _____
16. _____	36. _____	56. _____
17. _____	37. _____	57. _____
18. _____	38. _____	58. _____
19. _____	39. _____	59. _____
20. _____	40. _____	60. _____

(DIRECTIONS FOR SOLVING THREEZIES ARE ON PAGE 120)

Margarine

There are at least 59 words, each of four letters or more, that can be made out of the letters in the word MARGARINE.

1. _____	21. _____	40. _____
2. _____	22. _____	41. _____
3. _____	23. _____	42. _____
4. _____	24. _____	43. _____
5. _____	25. _____	44. _____
6. _____	26. _____	45. _____
7. _____	27. _____	46. _____
8. _____	28. _____	47. _____
9. _____	29. _____	48. _____
10. _____	30. _____	49. _____
11. _____	31. _____	50. _____
12. _____	32. _____	51. _____
13. _____	33. _____	52. _____
14. _____	34. _____	53. _____
15. _____	35. _____	54. _____
16. _____	36. _____	55. _____
17. _____	37. _____	56. _____
18. _____	38. _____	57. _____
19. _____	39. _____	58. _____
20. _____		59. _____

Seraglio

There are at least 57 words that can be made out of the letters in the word SERAGLIO.

1. _____
2. _____
3. _____
4. _____
5. _____
6. _____
7. _____
8. _____
9. _____
10. _____
11. _____
12. _____
13. _____
14. _____
15. _____
16. _____
17. _____
18. _____
19. _____
20. _____
21. _____
22. _____

23. _____
24. _____
25. _____
26. _____
27. _____
28. _____
29. _____
30. _____
31. _____
32. _____
33. _____
34. _____
35. _____
36. _____
37. _____
38. _____
39. _____
40. _____
41. _____
42. _____
43. _____
44. _____

45. _____
46. _____
47. _____
48. _____
49. _____
50. _____
51. _____
52. _____
53. _____
54. _____
55. _____
56. _____
57. _____

(DIRECTIONS FOR SOLVING ALFABITS ARE ON PAGE 102)

Singularly

There are at least 55 words, each of four or more letters, that can be made out of the letters in the word SINGULARLY.

1. _____
2. _____
3. _____
4. _____
5. _____
6. _____
7. _____
8. _____
9. _____
10. _____
11. _____
12. _____
13. _____
14. _____
15. _____
16. _____
17. _____
18. _____
19. _____
20. _____
21. _____
22. _____
23. _____
24. _____
25. _____
26. _____
27. _____
28. _____
29. _____
30. _____
31. _____
32. _____
33. _____
34. _____
35. _____
36. _____
37. _____
38. _____
39. _____
40. _____
41. _____
42. _____
43. _____
44. _____
45. _____
46. _____
47. _____
48. _____
49. _____
50. _____
51. _____
52. _____
53. _____
54. _____
55. _____

Dandelions

There are at least 91 words of four letters or more that can be made out of the letters in the word DANDELIONS.

If you find 50, give yourself a posy; 65 is just dandy; and 80 makes you the Alfabit king.

1. _____	22. _____	43. _____
2. _____	23. _____	44. _____
3. _____	24. _____	45. _____
4. _____	25. _____	46. _____
5. _____	26. _____	47. _____
6. _____	27. _____	48. _____
7. _____	28. _____	49. _____
8. _____	29. _____	50. _____
9. _____	30. _____	51. _____
10. _____	31. _____	52. _____
11. _____	32. _____	53. _____
12. _____	33. _____	54. _____
13. _____	34. _____	55. _____
14. _____	35. _____	56. _____
15. _____	36. _____	57. _____
16. _____	37. _____	58. _____
17. _____	38. _____	59. _____
18. _____	39. _____	60. _____
19. _____	40. _____	61. _____
20. _____	41. _____	62. _____
21. _____	42. _____	63. _____

(DIRECTIONS FOR SOLVING ALFABITS ARE ON PAGE 102)

64._____   73._____   83._____

65._____   74._____   84._____

66._____   75._____   85._____

67._____   76._____   86._____

68._____   77._____   87._____

69._____   78._____   88._____

70._____   79._____   89._____

71._____   80._____   90._____

72._____   81._____   91._____

82._____

Genealogy

There are at least 25 words of four or more letters that can be made out of the letters in the word GENEALOGY.

A score of 13 shows seeds of thought; 17 indicates innate ability; and 21 means you're descended from geniuses.

1._____   9._____   18._____

2._____   10._____   19._____

3._____   11._____   20._____

4._____   12._____   21._____

5._____   13._____   22._____

6._____   14._____   23._____

7._____   15._____   24._____

8._____   16._____   25._____

17._____

(DIRECTIONS FOR SOLVING ALFABITS ARE ON PAGE 102)

Matrimonial

There are at least 85 words of four letters or more that can be made out of the word MATRIMONIAL.

A score of 50 displays talent; 65 is testimonial of excellence; and 75 makes you more than a "match" for this one!

1. _____	22. _____	43. _____
2. _____	23. _____	44. _____
3. _____	24. _____	45. _____
4. _____	25. _____	46. _____
5. _____	26. _____	47. _____
6. _____	27. _____	48. _____
7. _____	28. _____	49. _____
8. _____	29. _____	50. _____
9. _____	30. _____	51. _____
10. _____	31. _____	52. _____
11. _____	32. _____	53. _____
12. _____	33. _____	54. _____
13. _____	34. _____	55. _____
14. _____	35. _____	56. _____
15. _____	36. _____	57. _____
16. _____	37. _____	58. _____
17. _____	38. _____	59. _____
18. _____	39. _____	60. _____
19. _____	40. _____	61. _____
20. _____	41. _____	62. _____
21. _____	42. _____	63. _____

(DIRECTIONS FOR SOLVING ALFABITS ARE ON PAGE 102)

64. _____ 71. _____ 79. _____
65. _____ 72. _____ 80. _____
66. _____ 73. _____ 81. _____
67. _____ 74. _____ 82. _____
68. _____ 75. _____ 83. _____
69. _____ 76. _____ 84. _____
70. _____ 77. _____ 85. _____
78. _____

Statutory

There are at least 39 words of four or more letters that can be made out of the letters in the word STATUTORY.

A score of 20 is good; 28 certifies verbal skill; and 35 decrees you an expert.

1. _____ 14. _____ 27. _____
2. _____ 15. _____ 28. _____
3. _____ 16. _____ 29. _____
4. _____ 17. _____ 30. _____
5. _____ 18. _____ 31. _____
6. _____ 19. _____ 32. _____
7. _____ 20. _____ 33. _____
8. _____ 21. _____ 34. _____
9. _____ 22. _____ 35. _____
10. _____ 23. _____ 36. _____
11. _____ 24. _____ 37. _____
12. _____ 25. _____ 38. _____
13. _____ 26. _____ 39. _____

(DIRECTIONS FOR SOLVING ALFABITS ARE ON PAGE 102)   119

How to Solve Threezies

You are given a sequence of three letters. List all the words you can think of which contain these three letters *in exact sequence.*

The sequence may seem quite unlikely. For example, a sequence of letters R R H at first blush might seem completely hopeless, yet with a little thought you may come up with the words *catarrh* and *myrrh.* If the given three letters were M B S, you might find that out of this strange sequence you can form the words *numbskull* and *tombstone.*

The rules of the game are very simple. You may use only one form of the word. For example, if the threezie were N D L, a proper answer would be HANDLE. But then you couldn't use the words HANDLES, HANDLED, or HANDLING, since all these words are forms of the same root. However, where the words have a completely different usage, then they may both be used even though the roots are similar. Thus, since FOND is an adjective and FONDLE is a verb, you could score with the word FONDLY and also with the word FONDLE.

Proper names are off limits; hyphenated words are allowed.

If you can provide 50% of the words asked for, you're doing well; 65%, you're doing superbly; 80% or better makes you the *crème de la crème.*

A R F

There are at least 13 words which contain the letter sequence A R F.

1. _____   5. _____   10. _____

2. _____   6. _____   11. _____

3. _____   7. _____   12. _____

4. _____   8. _____   13. _____

                       9. _____

O K E

There are at least 30 words which contain the letter sequence O K E.

1. _____
2. _____
3. _____
4. _____
5. _____
6. _____
7. _____
8. _____
9. _____
10. _____

11. _____
12. _____
13. _____
14. _____
15. _____
16. _____
17. _____
18. _____
19. _____
20. _____

21. _____
22. _____
23. _____
24. _____
25. _____
26. _____
27. _____
28. _____
29. _____
30. _____

B O T

There are at least 14 words which contain the letter sequence B O T.

1. _____
2. _____
3. _____
4. _____
5. _____

6. _____
7. _____
8. _____
9. _____

10. _____
11. _____
12. _____
13. _____
14. _____

M E T

There are at least 36 words which contain the letter sequence M E T .

1. _____   13. _____   25. _____
2. _____   14. _____   26. _____
3. _____   15. _____   27. _____
4. _____   16. _____   28. _____
5. _____   17. _____   29. _____
6. _____   18. _____   30. _____
7. _____   19. _____   31. _____
8. _____   20. _____   32. _____
9. _____   21. _____   33. _____
10. _____   22. _____   34. _____
11. _____   23. _____   35. _____
12. _____   24. _____   36. _____

O L I

There are at least 51 words which contain the letter sequence O L I.

1. _____   5. _____   9. _____
2. _____   6. _____   10. _____
3. _____   7. _____   11. _____
4. _____   8. _____   12. _____

(DIRECTIONS FOR SOLVING THREEZIES ARE ON PAGE 120)

13. _____ 26. _____ 39. _____
14. _____ 27. _____ 40. _____
15. _____ 28. _____ 41. _____
16. _____ 29. _____ 42. _____
17. _____ 30. _____ 43. _____
18. _____ 31. _____ 44. _____
19. _____ 32. _____ 45. _____
20. _____ 33. _____ 46. _____
21. _____ 34. _____ 47. _____
22. _____ 35. _____ 48. _____
23. _____ 36. _____ 49. _____
24. _____ 37. _____ 50. _____
25. _____ 38. _____ 51. _____

ERG

There are at least 20 words which contain the letter sequence E R G.

1. _____   8. _____ 14. _____
2. _____   9. _____ 15. _____
3. _____ 10. _____ 16. _____
4. _____ 11. _____ 17. _____
5. _____ 12. _____ 18. _____
6. _____ 13. _____ 19. _____
7. _____   20. _____

(DIRECTIONS FOR SOLVING THREEZIES ARE ON PAGE 120)

P T A

There are at least 12 words which contain the letter sequence P T A.
A score of 4 is good; 7 or more is capital.

1. _____   5. _____   9. _____
2. _____   6. _____   10. _____
3. _____   7. _____   11. _____
4. _____   8. _____   12. _____

S U M

There are at least 21 words which contain the letter sequence S U M.
A score of 10 is fine; 13 is grand; and 15 is *summa cum laude*.

1. _____   8. _____   15. _____
2. _____   9. _____   16. _____
3. _____   10. _____   17. _____
4. _____   11. _____   18. _____
5. _____   12. _____   19. _____
6. _____   13. _____   20. _____
7. _____   14. _____   21. _____

(DIRECTIONS FOR SOLVING THREEZIES ARE ON PAGE 120)

N G E

At least 65 words contain the letter sequence NGE. How many can you list? A score of 33 is commendable; 45, laudatory; and 57 brings highest encomiums.

1. _____	23. _____	44. _____
2. _____	24. _____	45. _____
3. _____	25. _____	46. _____
4. _____	26. _____	47. _____
5. _____	27. _____	48. _____
6. _____	28. _____	49. _____
7. _____	29. _____	50. _____
8. _____	30. _____	51. _____
9. _____	31. _____	52. _____
10. _____	32. _____	53. _____
11. _____	33. _____	54. _____
12. _____	34. _____	55. _____
13. _____	35. _____	56. _____
14. _____	36. _____	57. _____
15. _____	37. _____	58. _____
16. _____	38. _____	59. _____
17. _____	39. _____	60. _____
18. _____	40. _____	61. _____
19. _____	41. _____	62. _____
20. _____	42. _____	63. _____
21. _____	43. _____	64. _____
22. _____		65. _____

(DIRECTIONS FOR SOLVING THREEZIES ARE ON PAGE 120)

ARD

We found 71 words which contain the letter sequence ARD. How many can you fill in?

A score of 35 is fine; 48 is terrific; and 62—felicitations, paRDner!

1. _____	22. _____	43. _____
2. _____	23. _____	44. _____
3. _____	24. _____	45. _____
4. _____	25. _____	46. _____
5. _____	26. _____	47. _____
6. _____	27. _____	48. _____
7. _____	28. _____	49. _____
8. _____	29. _____	50. _____
9. _____	30. _____	51. _____
10. _____	31. _____	52. _____
11. _____	32. _____	53. _____
12. _____	33. _____	54. _____
13. _____	34. _____	55. _____
14. _____	35. _____	56. _____
15. _____	36. _____	57. _____
16. _____	37. _____	58. _____
17. _____	38. _____	59. _____
18. _____	39. _____	60. _____
19. _____	40. _____	61. _____
20. _____	41. _____	62. _____
21. _____	42. _____	63. _____

(DIRECTIONS FOR SOLVING THREEZIES ARE ON PAGE 120)

64. _____   67. _____   69. _____

65. _____   68. _____   70. _____

66. _____   71. _____

C L E

There are at least 43 words with the letter sequence CLE. How many can you find?

A score of 20 is very good; 28 is excellent; and 36 is spectacular.

1. _____	15. _____	30. _____
2. _____	16. _____	31. _____
3. _____	17. _____	32. _____
4. _____	18. _____	33. _____
5. _____	19. _____	34. _____
6. _____	20. _____	35. _____
7. _____	21. _____	36. _____
8. _____	22. _____	37. _____
9. _____	23. _____	38. _____
10. _____	24. _____	39. _____
11. _____	25. _____	40. _____
12. _____	26. _____	41. _____
13. _____	27. _____	42. _____
14. _____	28. _____	43. _____
	29. _____	

(DIRECTIONS FOR SOLVING THREEZIES ARE ON PAGE 120)   127

Crossword Puzzle No. 1

ACROSS

1. Spheres
5. Discoloration
10. Continued pain
14. Ditch
15. Great artery
16. Unruffled
17. Autocracy; despotism
19. Select
20. Followed backward
21. Rectifies
23. Imitated
24. Sow
25. Elevations
28. Thrilling
31. Spirit of the air
32. Oceans
33. One of the Cyclades
34. Footlike part
35. Somewhat tart
38. Damage
39. Advance by small degrees
41. Chief
42. Uplift
44. Misleading
46. Hoisted
47. Aromatic herb
48. Variegated
49. Forms in a row
51. Thinnest
55. Fruit
56. Unfeeling
58. Prophet
59. Sheer fabric
60. Mint
61. Advantage
62. Consumer
63. Extremities

DOWN

1. Persian poet
2. Garment
3. Woody fiber
4. Safekeeping of goods
5. Dressings
6. Carried: colloq.
7. Dry
8. Possessive pronoun
9. Undistinguished
10. Stresses
11. Compatriot
12. Retain
13. Cloth measures
18. Revers
22. Scottish prefix to names
24. Manifest
25. Swift
26. Goddess of peace

27. Repudiated
28. Weird
29. Angry
30. Minded
32. Urbane
36. Leaving out
37. Wading birds
40. Craves
43. Framework of crossed strips
45. Offense

46. Hunter
48. Ascend
49. Besides
50. Prevaricated
51. Narrow shoal
52. Black
53. Glided
54. Numbers
57. Extinct bird

Crossword Puzzle No. 2

ACROSS

1. Culture medium
5. Circular roof
9. Manufactured
13. Word expressing action
17. Donated
18. Wicked
19. Baking chamber
20. Jewish month
21. Precious stone
22. The sky
24. Plexus
25. Animal jelly
27. Checked
29. Prong
30. Cotton seeder
31. Auction
32. Irony
35. Mountain crest
37. Little lump
41. Over
42. Seed covering
43. Speed contest
45. Gender
46. Easy gait
47. Candid

48. Kind of cheese
49. Undulate
50. Citrus drink
51. Level
52. Lump of turf
53. Bet
54. Mock
56. Abominate
58. Amuse
59. Dreadful
61. Illuminated
62. Surrender
63. Pierced
67. Tear
71. Virginia willow
72. Wander about
74. Angered
75. Expense
76. Act
77. So be it
78. Require
79. Poker stake
80. Terminates
81. Saucy
82. Smelling or tasting strong

DOWN

1. Eager
2. Yawn
3. Of grandparents
4. Kinsman

5. Describe nature of
6. Sheeplike
7. Mud
8. Shade tree

9. Instant
10. The birds
11. Small depressions
12. Access
13. Altered
14. Paradise
15. Value
16. Reared
23. Spirit of the air
26. Become weary
28. Lilylike plant
30. Broad smile
32. Dish of greens
33. Dwelling

34. Shark (Eur.)
35. Boxing ring
36. Mistake
38. Custom
39. Device used as a pry
40. Put forth effort
42. Monkey
44. Assist
47. Annul
48. Stain
49. Faltering
51. Revise
52 Scold
53. Broad

55. Conceive
57. Mixes
58. Decorous
60. Corroded
62. Purvey food
63. Size of type
64. Short jacket
65. Cozy residence
66. Made an equal score
67. Hobbling
68. Extent
69. Be full
70. Whirlpool
73. Knock

Crossword Puzzle No. 3

ACROSS

1. Small valley
5. On the ocean
9. In a line
13. Trimming
17. Frank
18. Farm building
19. Cipher
20. Winglike
21. Not so much
22. Act of shunning
24. Bulk
25. Performs
27. Ancient town in Italy
28. Place again
29. Single things
30. Simmer
31. Males
32. Endures
35. Entreaty
36. Remote
40. Instant
41. Division of time
42. Mislaid
43. Evergreen tree
44. Tranquility
45. Recalls
47. Rodents
48. Wire measure
49. Soft part of fruit
50. Electrified particles
51. Transportation prices
52. Hardened
54. Finishes
55. Joins at an angle
56. Drowse
57. Great Lake
58. Daughter of Eurytus in mythology
59. Dampen
62. Sea-swallow
63. Current
67. Maple genus
68. Haughtiness
70. Title
71. Rough coat of hair
72. Den
73. Frenchman
74. So be it!
75. Sacred
76. Scrutinizes
77. Possessive pronoun
78. Loan

DOWN

1. Meadow mouse
2. Highest point
3. .... majesty
4. Fix comfortably

132

5. Lessens
6. Rescues
7. God of love
8. Tropical cuckoo
9. Flowering shrub
10. Renovate
11. Killer whale
12. Grief
13. Deplore
14. Alackaday!
15. Circumstance
16. Formerly (arch.)
23. Deciding
26. Wavy in heraldry
28. Remainder
30. Large number

31. Lose
32. Stalks
33. Characteristic
34. Passageway
35. Splendor
36. June beetles
37. In flames
38. Finer
39. Lock of hair
41. Possessed
42. Optical glass
45. Regretted
46. Portend
47. Motherly
49. Farm implement
51. Rasp

53. Vigor
54. Mistakes
55. Patterns
57. Weird
58. Bring upon oneself
59. Party
60. Reverberate
61. Apportion
62. Server
63. Two-toed sloth
64. Docile
65. Sign
66. Proceed
68. Malt beverage
69. Past

Crossword Puzzle No. 4

ACROSS

1. Bin
5. Object of blind sacrifice
15. California rock fish
16. Fickle
17. Pernicious
18. Imbibe
19. Project
20. Cupola
21. Secures
22. Bestow
23. River in Asia
24. Lip in a casting ladle
25. Remunerate
26. Instruct
28. Condemn
30. Knight
33. Of a remote ancestor
35. Pair
36. Silver coin
37. Having two hydrogen atoms

39. Settles in temporary habitations
41. Relax
42. Roam idly
44. In abundance
45. Compass point
46. City in Massachusetts
48. Made of flax
49. Personal pronoun
50. Small bottle
52. Cult adherent
53. Addition
56. Liquid measure
57. Heddles of a loom
58. Skate genus
59. Incensed
60. Land measure
61. Blasphemer
63. Shower
64. Bestowal
65. Intrigue

DOWN

1. Worthy
2. Circuit
3. Unique
4. Bundle
5. Critic
6. Illiterate
7. Ground

8. Roman clan
9. Large deer
10. Japanese distance measure
11. Shaggy
12. Talented
13. Prussian lancer: var.
14. Incline

134

22. Declare
24. Gray: Fr.
25. Fork
27. Ellipsoidal
29. Intimation
30. Pertaining to traffic in sacred things
31. Concert manager
32. Indignation
34. Roll of tobacco
36. Surrealist painter
38. Wolframite
40. Summon

43. Wander
46. Harden
47. Author of "Paradise Lost"
49. Vital organ
51. Brisk
53. Part of the eye
54. Designate
55. Drank slowly: rare
56. Metric weight
57. Find fault
59. Dessert
62. Hebrew deity

Crossword Puzzle No. 5

ACROSS

1. Baseballer Hornsby
6. Lights out!
10. A helluva state to be in
14. Entertain
15. Hodgepodge
16. Giant corn bin
17. He of the Golden Touch
18. A size; a card; a fish
19. A backward citrus
20. Investigate
21. Frigid
23. Conceit
25. To make out by laborious means
26. Bend
28. Habituates
30. Restate
33. Immense expanse: unlimited quantity
35. Happening
36. Resorts
37. Cooled
41. Pekoe or Earl Grey
42. Afterward (archaic)
44. Possessive pronoun

46. Sinatra's former wife
47. Irish Gaelic
49. The chief product of the Hawaiian Islands
51. Diminish
53. Blusters
55. Passionate
56. Hostile
59. Female zebras
61. Epoch
62. Flightless bird
64. Spelled backward it means to catch
65. Author of *Maelzel's Chessplayer*
68. Ominous
70. Old Testament character
72. "Beulah, peel me a _____." Mae West
74. Famous lioness
75. Catches
76. Summation of factors
77. Afghan unit of weight
78. Woody perennial
79. Ropes by the hind feet

DOWN

1. Sloping floor
2. Arabian nobleman (Var. sp.)
3. Girl's name
4. King of Judah
5. Vacillate

6. World's largest city
7. Cassius Clay
8. Languish
9. Most sodden
10. Service

11. Track official
12. Similar
13. Nothing at all, but you can break your neck in them
22. Half-baked bed
24. Fuegian Indian
26. Oriental coin
27. Father
29. Single (prefix)
30. Network
31. On any occasion
32. Black-eyed or chick
34. Old Testament character
36. Luminary
38. Part of toreador's apparatus
39. Nicely balanced
40. Tapered seam
43. Piece

45. Brawn
48. Very (Greek form comb.)
50. Doctrine; cause; theory
52. Notices
54. Unit
55. Genus of macaws
56. Location of River Styx
57. Fast
58. Short
60. Vituperation
63. Consumer
65. Head
66. Gem
67. Fish
69. Piece of corn
71. Consumed
73. Deer

Crossword Puzzle No. 6

ACROSS

1. Offhand; extemporaneous
10. Steep slope
15. Tuneful
16. Sot
17. Too early
18. Swiss copper coin
19. Cleche: heraldry
20. Sea bird
21. Despotic subordinate official
22. Touch: Scot.
23. Lentiginous
25. Wood sorrel
26. Run away to be married
28. Genus including frogs
29. Ended
30. Eastern Aramaic dialect
32. Small pet dog
34. Emperor
36. Occident
37. Phantoms
41. Stings
45. Eldest son of Ham
46. Charts
48. Wide-awake
49. Injure by exposure
50. Matrimonial
52. Evergreen tree
53. Crystalline alkaloid
55. Wolframite
56. The third power
57. Hinge
58. Index
60. A flat fold
61. Expiation
62. Shrieks
63. Induces

DOWN

1. Attributes
2. Blithely
3. Promisor (var.)
4. Italian city
5. Harem room
6. Episcopal crown
7. Server of tea
8. Revolving chimney device
9. Avail oneself of
10. Wander
11. Outer garment
12. Ratify
13. Retraces steps
14. Make ready
21. Moderates
23. Banquet
24. Recognized
27. Throw

29. Noumenal
31. Railway conductor
33. Pertaining to a doctrine
35. Posterior
37. Fragmentary
38. Childish
39. Of the summer
40. Furnish with spikes
42. Sought protection

43. Raised platform
44. Thoroughfares
47. Motor part
50. Baseball gloves
51. Hunting dogs
54. Wind spirally
56. Stupor
58. Acme
59. Rumanian coin

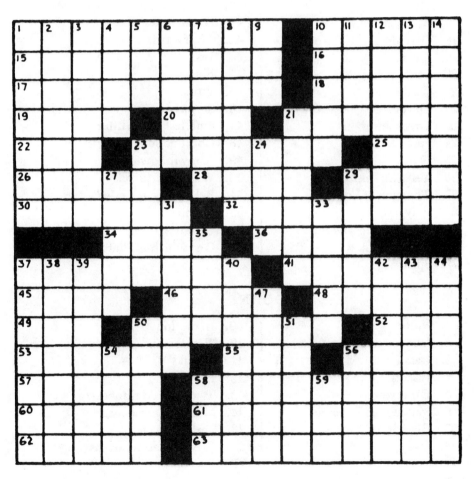

Crossword Puzzle No. 7

ACROSS

1. Word group
7. Political symbol in form of Greek cross
15. Checked, controlled
16. Hurrier
17. Make a speech
18. River in South Carolina
19. Exists
20. Soaks
21. Outlaw
22. Devoured
23. Greek letter
24. Intersection
25. Oven
26. Yes in Spanish
27. The twin of Pollux
28. Polynesian group
29. City in Pennsylvania
31. Breakfast food
32. Spirit
33. Fun
34. City in Ohio
36. Intentions
39. Performer
40. Slices
41. Greek letter
42. Afterwards
43. List
44. Flap
45. Pronoun
46. Stopped
47. Smallest of the litter
48. Conjunction
49. Army follower
50. Watercourse
51. Relating to a landed estate
53. Revolve
54. Ordainers
55. One who humiliates

DOWN

1. Valor
2. Unorthodox religionist
3. Lasso
4. Insects
5. Observe
6. Masculine nickname
7. River in Ireland
8. Stray
9. In motion
10. "Let it stand"
11. Mound
12. Preposition
13. Two-horned rhinoceros
14. Military storehouse
18. Tailor: Latin
21. City in Massachusetts

22. Gun pointers
24. Frankness
25. African tablelands
27. Pasteboard box
28. Always: Latin
30. Raver
31. Bent
33. Causer of pain
34. Negative electrode
35. River of Woe
36. Crayons

37. Issue
38. Craftier
40. Neckband
43. Proportion
44. Prickly pears
46. Search
47. Pro _____
49. Pouch
50. Male swan
52. Parent: colloq.
53. Sun god

Crossword Puzzle No. 8

ACROSS

1. What felled Adam
6. Peruse lightly
10. Chief performer
14. Ventured
15. Punish by whacking
16. One who is too afraid to run away
17. A co-opera
18. Squander
19. Consumes
20. Female suffix
21. Central or Hyde
22. Ornate
24. Fate
26. List of candidates
27. Finish
28. Leaks
29. Prefix meaning to reverse
31. Fabricates
34. Something that's rarely clear
35. Question word
36. Need
37. Phones
38. V
39. Noah's boat
40. A man who is here today and here tomorrow (pl.)
41. Pumpkin eater
42. I
43. Tunnels
44. Payable
45. Notes
46. In good condition (2 words)
50. These outrank hearts
52. Dispose of
53. Rita or Grande
54. Block of congealed matter
55. Flower holder of the gay 90's
57. "After the _____" Arthur Miller
58. Grows old
59. Man's greatest invention (2 words)
60. Scorned
61. A musical notation
62. Espouses
63. Lock

DOWN

1. Augmented
2. Stop
3. Newspapers
4. Allow
5. Past suffix
6. Alarming
7. "The _____ of Amontillado." (Poe)
8. Symbol of industriousness
9. Without good purpose
10. Linens or paper
11. Vex
12. _____ and crafts
13. Very promising
18. Stick
21. Bowling objects

23. Carried away
25. Tepee
26. Ornamental stamps
28. Parts of shoes or fish
29. Peacenik
30. Jug
31. Indian pundit who has lost his ego
32. Peel
33. Waterman's or Carter's
34. Worries
35. Struck
37. Massacred cabbage
38. Know by touch
40. Study hard
41. Handle
43. Not excessive
44. Where, as children, we first met the farmer
45. Appropriates
46. A plant, as Emerson put it, whose virtues have not been discovered (pl.)
47. Declaim
48. Puts in order
49. Creases
50. A lasting effect of a disturbing experience
51. Personal attendant of a noble
52. Rushed
56. Fortas or Attel
57. Dolce _____ niente
60. Altitude (abbr.)

Crossword Puzzle No. 9

ACROSS

1. Behave
4. What you need at a seance
7. Spread through
14. Entwine
16. Tallow constituent
17. Real estate broker
18. Fall seasons
19. Canary color
20. Pet name for a certain car
21. Babylonian god of the sky
22. Disgrace
24. River in Germany
25. Attain
30. Collector of income taxes
31. Signal light
32. Stresses
34. Beverage
35. Changed

36. Cried like a frog
40. Charge
41. Adorn
42. Declined
45. Preserve fruit
46. French annuity
47. Meadows
48. Great artery
50. Nocturnal bird
51. Burden
52. Nettled: colloq.
58. Talky talk
60. Upstart
61. Corrosive
62. Messengers' calls
63. Sharp replies
64. Weights (abbr.)
65. Inquire

DOWN

1. Askew
2. Algonquin Indian
3. River duck
4. Ending for palm- or fals-
5. Demonstrates
6. For each
7. Hymns
8. Musical study
9. Prepares flax
10. Vauxhall (abbr.)
11. Fleet of warships

12. Principal meal
13. Render safe
15. Total
20. Paddles
23. Hastened
24. Ester of oleic acid
25. Remainder (abbr.)
26. Australian bird
27. Pertinent
28. Wears by friction
29. Despised

31. Finely ground meal
33. Perceive
34. Constellation
36. Penny
37. Relative
38. Newt
39. Coloring matter
41. Obstructs
42. Marital fugitive
43. Take care
44. Election ticket
45. Woos
48. Concerning (arch.)
49. Separated
51. Above
53. Bungles
54. Feminine name
55. Vein: Lat.
56. Terminates
57. Gloom
59. Hue and cry
60. Bench in a church

Crossword Puzzle No 10

ACROSS

1. Comprehend
6. Voucher for small sum
10. Nonsense! (slang)
14. Tag
15. Competition
16. Part
17. Rugged crest
18. Grade School (abbr.)
19. Insignificant part
20. To explode
22. Went by
24. Secure
25. Mail
26. Turn back
29. Word of mouth
30. Diminutive suffix
31. Time periods
33. To wane
37. Chant
39. Disturbances

41. Portion
42. Diner
44. Deities of art
46. Nothing
47. Muffled
49. Delicate management
51. Complained
54. Mahometan Filipino
55. Citrus fruit
56. Sneering
60. Hebrew law
61. Post
63. Winged
64. Entrance to a mine
65. Rim
66. Splits
67. _____ Majesty
68. Puts on
69. Appears

DOWN

1. Joyous
2. Uncommon
3. Uphold
4. Bristly
5. Entire
6. Greek island
7. Hearty
8. Chill
9. Assuage

10. Stiff hairs
11. Unfastened
12. Change
13. Leads
21. Following
23. Above
25. Endures
26. Artifice
27. Charles Lamb

28. Outlet
29. Haughty
32. Pointed
34. Sound
35. Send out
36. Trust
38. Arrange in pairs
40. Spanish gentleman
43. Crossbar
45. Native chiefs in India
48. Abounded

50. Oriental laborer
51. Relating to wheels
52. Wear away
53. City of Light
54. Men
56. Symbol
57. Wheel hub
58. Article
59. Tax
62. Fuss

Crossword Puzzle No. 11

ACROSS

1. Legwear
5. By mouth
9. Feel pain
14. "Somewhere _____ the Rainbow"
15. Costume
16. White bruin
17. Nobleman
18. Composition for two
19. Superior
20. Black fluid
21. Stake
22. Rocky peak
24. Barnyard fowl
25. Distant
27. A muffin made of coarse flour
28. Smoothe
29. Propose
31. Placid
33. Companion
34. Weed
35. Hegemon
39. Wrath

40. Café dansant
42. "All About _____"
43. Fright
45. Repartee
46. Exposed
47. Snare
49. Bestow
50. _____ rags
53. A spread in gin rummy
54. Stag
55. Sped
56. Exercise room
57. What Joshua did
58. Coke product
61. Remain
63. A cherub off the track
65. Sand hill
66. Place (2 words)
67. Fluff
68. Golf club
69. Not sterling
70. Snappish
71. Repair

DOWN

1. Pueblo Indian
2. Stove
3. Look for (2 words)
4. Sin

5. Monastic brotherhood
6. Scatter
7. Lincoln
8. Missive

9. Spelled backward it means knocks
10. Crowd
11. Hawaiian greeting
12. Poe's masterpiece
13. Drift
21. A counter that separates drinkers from their money
23. Egg preparation
26. Charge
27. Escape
28. "Break! Break! Break! On thy cold gray stones, O _____." (Tennyson)
29. Neglect
30. Taxi toll
31. Term of beratement
32. Gain after taxes
34. In some measure
36. Embarkment

37. Level
38. Torn
40. Man in stir
41. Tombstone abbr.
44. "_____ skies at morning"
46. Rough metal
48. Wander
49. Acquire
50. Grip
51. Tag
52. Santa _____
54. Light song
56. Former Senator McCarthy
57. Tooth
59. Soon
60. Curve
62. Speck
64. Disencumber
65. Vague

149

Crossword Puzzle No. 12

ACROSS

1. "_____, poor Yorick!"
5. Altar-end of church
9. On the level
14. Choice
16. Fragrance
17. Current
18. Slopes
19. Silkworm
20. One of the Araceae
22. Kitchen vessel
23. Routine task
26. River of the lower regions
27. Sea, to Caesar
28. Wander
29. Mineral spring
30. First president of the former German Republic
32. Serviceableness
33. Type of contract
35. Hatred
37. Ankle injuries
39. Manor house
41. Shy
42. One of the fifty
44. Shepherd's pipe
45. Claw
47. Opp. of subways
48. Grafted (her.)
49. Low
50. Hautboy
52. Constellation
53. On one's dignity
54. Masculine name
55. Thus (obs.)
56. Beleaguerment
58. Two-pronged
63. Silver citrate
64. High praise
65. Sacs
66. Austrian river
67. Snow vehicle

DOWN

1. Viper
2. Gaelic sea god
3. Beverage
4. Harsh
5. A king in the Volsunga Saga
6. A tattling gossip
7. Instrumental compositions
8. Admission
9. Fat
10. Babylonian war god
11. Parallels
12. Insistent
13. Savor
15. Solicitude

21. Chopping tool
23. Outer shell
24. Southern trait
25. Subjugates
26. Sudden convulsive action
27. Ancient Asian
29. Japanese coin
31. Swagger (prov. Eng.)
33. Italian beach
34. Roman magistrate
36. Unit of length
38. Winged (her.)
40. Entity

43. Wind harp
46. Name (Fr.)
48. Makes into law
49. Fundamental
51. The Scriptures
52. Electrical atmosphere
54. Lampreys
55. Soapy water
57. Secured
59. Mirth
60. Be indisposed
61. Digit
62. Conclusion

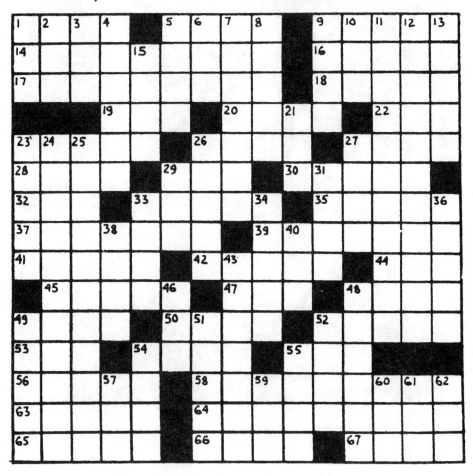

The "S" Quiz

The names of all of the 7 items pictured below begin with the letter "S," and the blanks beneath the pictures represent 1 letter each. How many can you identify?

A score of 4 is good; 6 is excellent; 7 is superb.

2. _ _ _ _ _ _ _

1. _ _ _ _ _ _ _ _ _ _

3. _ _ _ _ _ _

4. _ _ _ _ _ _ _

5. _ _ _ _ _ _ _ _ _ _

6. _ _ _ _ _ _ _ _ _

7. _ _ _ _ _ _ _ _ _ _

153

The "G" Quiz

The names of all of the 8 items pictured below begin with the letter "G," and the blanks beneath the pictures represent 1 letter each. How many can you identify?

A score of 5 is good; 7 is excellent; 8 is letter-perfect!

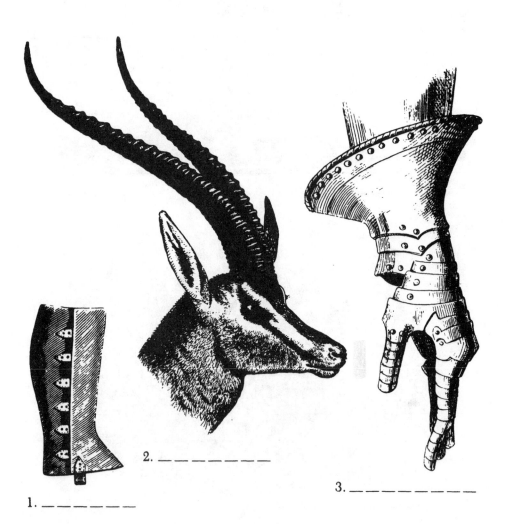

1. _ _ _ _ _ _

2. _ _ _ _ _ _ _

3. _ _ _ _ _ _ _ _ _

154

4. _ _ _ _ _ _ _

5. _ _ _ _ _ _ _ _ _ _ _ _

6. _ _ _ _ _ _

7. _ _ _ _ _ _ _ _ _

8. _ _ _ _ _ _ _ _

155

The "B" Quiz

The names of the things pictured in this test begin with the letter "B." Can you identify them? Use the number of blanks as a clue.

A score of 9 is good; 12 is better; a perfect 15 is the best it could be!

3. _ _ _ _ _

1. _ _ _ _ _ _ _

2. _ _ _ _ _ _ _ _

4. _ _ _ _ _ _ _

5. _ _ _ _ _ _ _ _ _

6. _ _ _ _ _ _ _

9. _ _ _ _ _ _ _ _

7. _ _ _ _ _ _ _

10. _ _ _ _ _ _ _

8. _ _ _ _ _

11. _ _ _ _ _

14. _ _ _ _ _ _ _ _ _

12. _ _ _ _ _ _ _ _

13. _ _ _ _ _

15. _ _ _ _ _ _

The "O" Quiz

All of the things pictured on these pages begin with the letter "O." Can you name them? The blanks beneath each picture tell you the number of letters in the word.

A score of 7 is OK; 11 is on target; all 13 is outstanding!

1. _ _ _ _ _ _ _ _ _ _ _ _

2. _ _ _ _ _ _ _

3. _ _ _ _ _ _ _ _ _ _

4. _ _ _ _ _ _

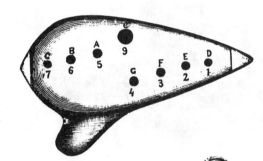

5. _ _ _ _ _ _ _

7. _ _ _ _ _ _ _ _

6. _ _ _ _ _ _

8. _ _ _ _ _ _ _

160

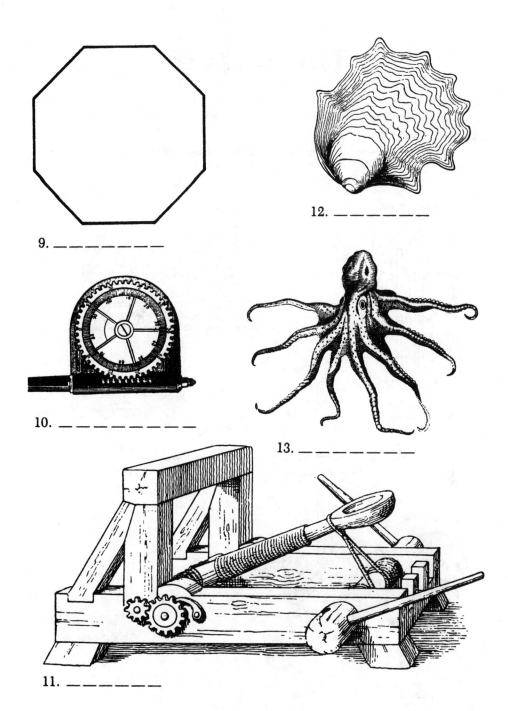

9. _ _ _ _ _ _ _

10. _ _ _ _ _ _ _

11. _ _ _ _ _ _

12. _ _ _ _ _ _ _

13. _ _ _ _ _ _ _

The L Quiz

Every one of the 15 items pictured here begins with the letter L. The dashes indicate the number of letters in each name. How many of them can you identify?

A score of 8 is lovely; 11 is laudable; and 12 is a lollapalooza!

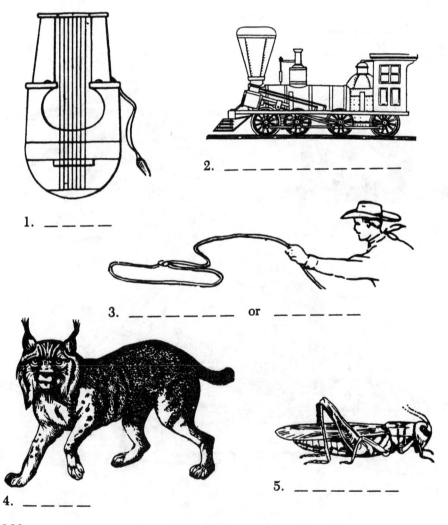

1. _ _ _ _ _

2. _ _ _ _ _ _ _ _ _ _ _

3. _ _ _ _ _ _ _   or   _ _ _ _ _ _

4. _ _ _ _

5. _ _ _ _ _ _

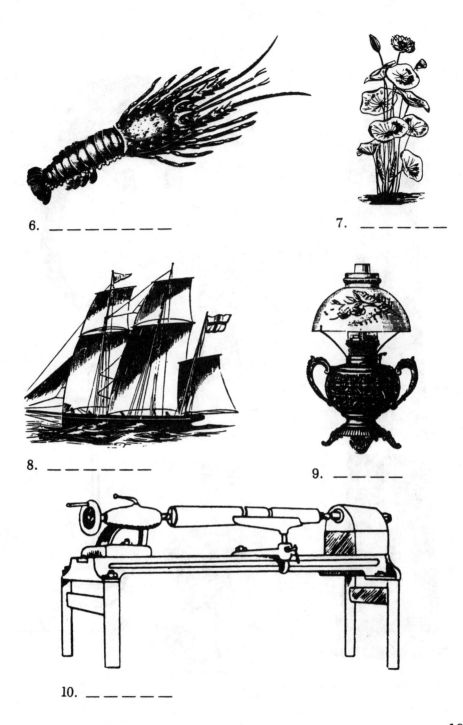

6. _ _ _ _ _ _ _

7. _ _ _ _ _

8. _ _ _ _ _ _ _

9. _ _ _ _ _

10. _ _ _ _ _

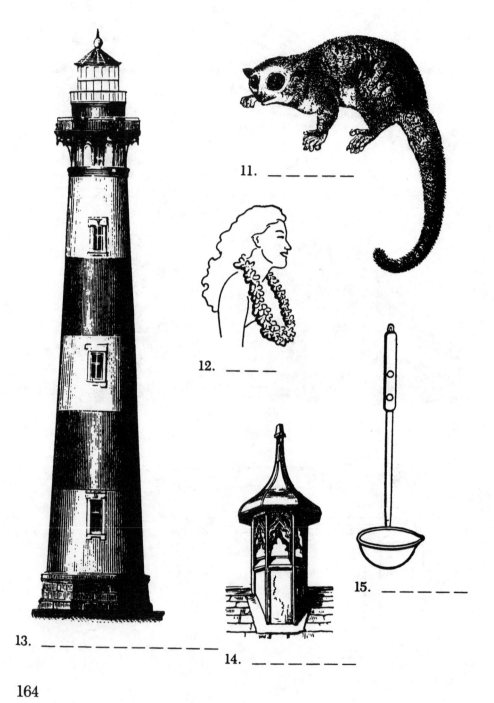

11. _ _ _ _ _ _

12. _ _ _ _

13. _ _ _ _ _ _ _ _ _ _ _

14. _ _ _ _ _ _ _

15. _ _ _ _ _ _

A Head for Figures

Although this test does take for granted a certain basic knowledge of arithmetic, it is in no sense an achievement test. It is designed to test your flair for mathematical reasoning rather than your knowledge of mathematical techniques and formulas.

Write your answer on the line provided before each question. Accuracy is more important than speed, but do not linger too long on any one question. You may do rough figuring in the margins or on a separate piece of paper.

Turn to the answer section to find out how to score yourself. A score of 15 is fair; 18 is good; 21 is superb; and if you score a perfect 24, well, you must have quite a head for figures!

TIME LIMIT: 40 MINUTES

_____ 1. If 4 apples out of a dozen are bad, how many are good?

_____ 2. In a box of 48 apples, 8 out of each dozen are good. How many in the box are bad?

_____ 3. What number is as much less than 60 as it is more than 50?

_____ 4. A girl spent half her money for apples and half that amount for milk, which left her with 40 cents. How much did she spend for the apples?

_____ 5. How many hours will it take a car to go 400 miles at a speed of 50 miles per hour?

_____ 6. 36 is as much more than 29 as it is less than what number?

_____ 7. Your watch gains 4 minutes in a 24-hour day. If it reads 7:30½ at 7:30 A.M., how fast will it be at actual noon of the same day?

8. The sum of A plus B equals 116. A is 3 less than C, but 4 more than B. What number does C equal?

9. If 7 men in 100 are criminals, how many men in 500 are not criminals?

10. Smith, a broker, bought 3 shares at 10 each which he sold at 6 each, and sold at 6 each what he bought at 5 each. If his total profit was 8, how many shares had he bought at 5?

11. How many hours will it take a jet plane to travel 400 miles at a speed of 600 miles per hour?

12. If 6½ yards of upholstery cloth cost 26 dollars, how much will 3½ yards cost?

13. If a grocer has enough eggs to last 300 customers 2 weeks, how long will the eggs last 400 customers?

14. Suppose A, B, and C are numbers. Suppose D is the sum of A, B, and C. In that case, would D minus A equal B plus C?

15. Suppose A and B are numbers. Suppose D is the difference between A and B. In that case, would D plus A equal B, if B is greater than A?

16. It takes 10 ships 10 days to use 10 tanks of oil. How many days will it take 1 ship to use 1 tank of oil?

17. In this series, what is the next number? 1, 1, 2, 6 . . . .

18. In a lot of 154 coats, there are 3 less white coats than red coats, but 5 more white coats than green coats. If all the coats are red, white, or green, how many red coats are there?

19. If page 5 of a 24-page newspaper is missing, what other pages must also be missing?

20. If a boy scout hiked 2 miles per hour up a hill and 6 miles per hour down the hill, what was his average speed for the entire trip?

21. Out of 100 coffee drinkers, 17 take it without cream or sugar, 50 take sugar and 40 do not use cream. How many drink their coffee with cream and sugar combined?

22. Suppose the letters in this multiplication problem are numbers, and each dash represents a missing letter. Supply the missing letters.

$$
\begin{array}{r}
5\_4 \\
\times\, C\,5 \\
\hline
2\_A\,Y \\
\_1\,F\,6 \\
\hline
\_\_4\,8\_ \\
\end{array}
$$

23. Supply the missing numbers in this multiplication problem.

$$
\begin{array}{r}
\_\_\_\_ \\
\times\, 6\_ \\
\hline
7\_5\,8\_ \\
\_\_\_\_\_ \\
\hline
\_\_\_\_\_2\,6 \\
\end{array}
$$

24. Suppose the letters in this multiplication problem are numbers. What number does each letter equal?

$$
\begin{array}{r}
F\,1\,F \\
\times\, 2\,E \\
\hline
6\,3\,C \\
D\,2\,D \\
\hline
D\,8\,B\,C \\
\end{array}
$$

167

Observation Test

There may not be anything wrong with your vision, but how observant are you? Here are 15 questions to test how carefully and accurately you perceive things. Write your answers in the blanks. Allow yourself 10 minutes to complete the test.

Give yourself 10 points for each correct answer. A score of 70 is passing fair; 100 shows you have a keen eye; and 120 or better makes you a veritable Sherlock Holmes.

1. How many surfaces does this object have?

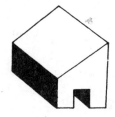

_____

_____

2. Which two figures are identical?

   (a)   (b)   (c)   (d)   (e)   (f)

_____

3. Which two figures are identical?

   (a)   (b)   (c)   (d)   (e)   (f)

168

4. Which two figures are identical?

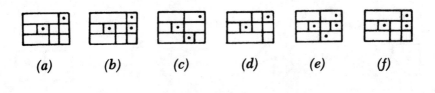

(a)   (b)   (c)   (d)   (e)   (f)

_____

5. Which two figures are identical?

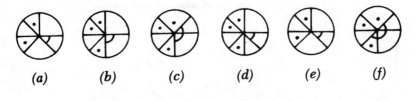

(a)   (b)   (c)   (d)   (e)   (f)

_____

6. How many surfaces does this figure have?

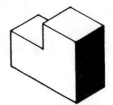

_____

_____

7.

P is to Q as K is to: _____

(a)   (b)   (c)   (d)

169

8.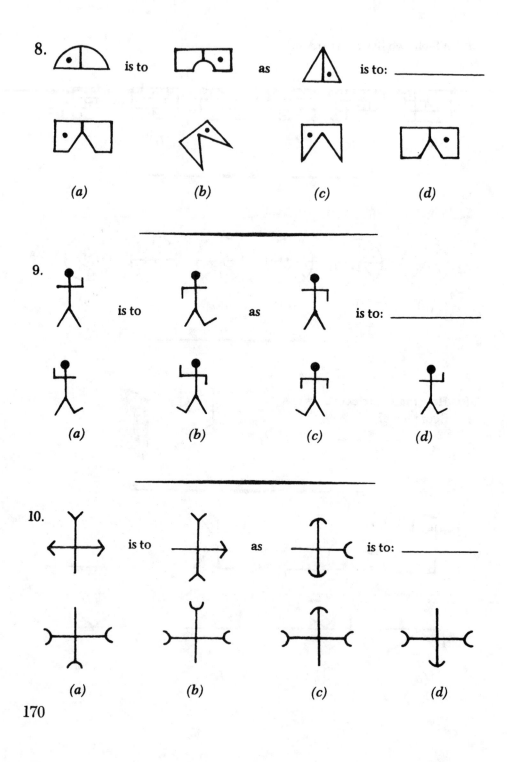

is to

as

is to: _____

(a) (b) (c) (d)

9.

is to

as

is to: _____

(a) (b) (c) (d)

10.

is to

as

is to: _____

(a) (b) (c) (d)

170

Questions 11–15 are based on the following figures:

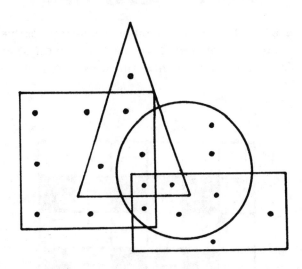

11. How many dots are in the triangle, but not in the circle?

   _____

12. How many dots are common to the rectangle, triangle, and circle?

   _____

13. How many dots are common to the circle, square, and triangle?

   _____

14. How many dots are common to the rectangle and square?

   _____

15. How many dots are common to all four figures: the square, the rectangle, the circle, and the triangle? _____

Mathecrostics

Here you have all the answers—you make up the problems. Fill each blank with a number from 1 to 9 so that the answers come out right for all the problems in the rows across and down. You may use a number more than once.

1.

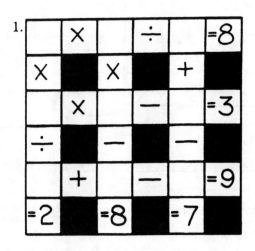

2.

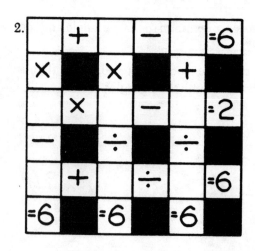

3.

	−		×		=6
×	■	×	■	+	■
	×		−		=2
÷	■	−	■	÷	■
	+		÷		=7
=2	■	=7	■	=5	■

5.

	+		÷		=8
+	■	−	■	×	■
	×		−		=6
−	■	×	■	÷	■
	−		−		=1
=5	■	=9	■	=4	■

4.

	×		−		=9
×	■	+	■	+	■
	+		÷		=2
−	■	−	■	÷	■
	+		−		=4
=7	■	=4	■	=2	■

6.

	÷		×		=8
×	■	+	■	×	■
	×		−		=6
÷	■	−	■	÷	■
	×		−		=8
=9	■	=1	■	=6	■

Vocabulary Quiz I

You have run across the 21 words in this quiz at one time or another in magazines, in books or in newspapers. Do you really know the meanings of these words? You have been given four choices; underline the definition you believe to be correct.

A score of 13 is passing, 17 is great, 20 is super duper.

1. ILLUSTRIOUS

    shiny *with pictures* *luminous* *famous*

2. STIPPLED

    speculated *spectacular* *speckled* *specious*

3. PROLIX

    tarry *talkative* *tabletop* *tall*

4. ALIEN

    French beer *foreign* *unhappy* *alone*

5. BASTION

    wooden club *large fish* *stronghold* *cant*

6. HYPERBOLE

    exaggeration *overeagerness* *overactivity* *champion bowler*

7. AUGMENT

    increment *influence* *increase* *incrustate*

8. PARSIMONIOUS

    green leafy vegetable *stingy* *healthful* *harmonious*

9. EQUIVOCAL

    ambiguous *outspoken* *equal* *riding bareback*

10. CADAVER

      scoundrel   *cavil*   *liver pate*   *corpse*

11. BROUHAHA

      hubbub   *elegant coach*   *college cheerleader*   *laughing gas*

12. FRACAS

      illness   *row*   *fog*   *Mexican pancake*

13. PUMMEL

      greasy kid stuff   *variety of apple*   *wordplay*   *beat*

14. HIATUS

      gap   *sap*   *lap*   *nap*

15. LAGNIAPPE

      precious metal   *ne'er-do-well*   *gratuity*   *siesta*

16. UKASE

      because   *opium derivative*   *edict*

      musical instrument resembling a guitar

17. PROTUBERANT

      enthusiastic   *bulging*   *positive*   *annoying*

18. PENCHANT

      neck medallion   *banner*   *predilection*   *prediction*

19. ECDYSIAST

      enthusiast   *stripteaser*   *dancer*   *one who studies echoes*

20. SATURNINE

      satirical   *sardonic*   *sullen*   *star-gazer*

21. DRACONIAN

      vampirelike   *harsh*   *monstrous*   *serpentine*

S E Quiz

The two letters, S E, appear in each of the five-letter words in this vocabulary quiz. The position of S E within the word is indicated, and the definition is given next to each word. Fill in the blanks to identify each word. Then check your answers.

A score of 16 is good, 19 is excellent, and 22 is exceptional.

Example: S E T U P   Plan; arrangement

1.   S E __ __ __   To wait on; meet the needs of

2.   S E __ __ __   Car for four or more persons

3.   S E __ __ __   To divide; separate; disjoin

4.   S E __ __ __   To feel; understand; perceive

5.   S E __ __ __   Brown pigment used in monochrome drawing

Example: E A S E L   Wooden frame to support a painting

6.   __ __ S E __   Avaricious person; hoarder of wealth

7.   __ __ S E __   To overturn; disturbed

8.   __ __ S E __   Something put within something else

9.   __ __ S E __   Inquisitive; prying

10.   __ __ S E __   Something with value; positive quality

Example: P H A S E   Stage; aspect of moon or planets

11. _ _ _ S E   To lift up; elevate; increase

12. _ _ _ S E   Slip of memory, tongue, or pen; slight mistake

13. _ _ _ S E   Apathetic; indifferent; bored

14. _ _ _ S E   Thick; impenetrable

15. _ _ _ S E   To rub out; obliterate

16. _ _ _ S E   Outdated

17. _ _ _ S E   Concise

18. _ _ _ S E   Ordinary speech or writing

Example: S A L V E   Healing ointment; to anoint

19. S _ _ _ E   Sword with a curved blade

20. S _ _ _ E   Horny plate; balance; instrument for weighing

21. S _ _ _ E   To move on ice; shoe with blade or roller

22. S _ _ _ E   To screen from light; make dark; cool place

23. S _ _ _ E   Large nail; sharp point; add liquor to a drink

24. S _ _ _ E   Move stealthily

Movie Memory

If you're a movie buff, this quiz should be child's play for you. Here are 26 major movies. For each movie, you are given a choice of three movie stars. The question is: Who played the lead in the movie named?

Mark your answer; then add up your score. If you got 16 right, you're allowed on the set; 19 gives you a starring role; and 22 puts you in the director's seat.

1. Separate Tables
   Noel Coward   *David Niven*   *Peter Sellers*

2. Night of the Iguana
   Cantinflas   *Laurence Harvey*   *Richard Burton*

3. The Producers
   Zero Mostel   *Sid Caesar*   *Woody Allen*

4. Blackboard Jungle
   Rock Hudson   *Glenn Ford*   *James Dean*

5. The Pawnbroker
   Sidney Poitier   *George C. Scott*   *Rod Steiger*

6. The Lost Weekend
   Ray Milland   *Paul Henreid*   *Peter Lorre*

7. Mutiny on the Bounty
   Richard Barthelmess   *Bela Lugosi*   *Charles Laughton*

8. The Three Faces of Eve
   Bette Davis   *Joanne Woodward*   *Myrna Loy*

9. National Velvet
   Shirley Temple   *Elizabeth Taylor*   *Freddie Bartholomew*

10. The Ipcress File
    Michael Caine   *Sean Connery*   *David Niven*

11. All the King's Men
    James Stewart   *Brian Donlevy*   *Broderick Crawford*

178

12. Cat Ballou
      George Kennedy   *Lee Marvin*   *Gary Cooper*

13. Suspicion
      Joan Fontaine   *Joan Caulfield*   *Joan Bennett*

14. The Jazz Singer
      Cab Calloway   *Al Jolson*   *Bing Crosby*

15. Tom Jones
      Albert Finney   *Richard Harris*   *Tom Courtenay*

16. Psycho
      Anthony Quinn   *Anthony Perkins*   *Anthony Quayle*

17. Love Story
      Ali MacGraw   *Sandy Dennis*   *Katharine Ross*

18. Papillon
      Steve McQueen   *Rock Hudson*   *George Segal*

19. A Touch of Class
      Faye Dunaway   *Estelle Parsons*   *Glenda Jackson*

20. Oh God!
      George Segal   *George Burns*   *George Gobel*

21. The Fox
      Sandy Duncan   *Sandy Dennis*   *Peter Sellers*

22. Slapshot
      Peter Fonda   *Michael Sarrazin*   *Paul Newman*

23. The Turning Point
      Anne Jackson   *Anne Bancroft*   *Ann Sothern*

24. Annie Hall
      Diane Canova   *Tuesday Weld*   *Diane Keaton*

25. Star Wars
      Marsha Mason   *Carrie Fisher*   *Teri Garr*

26. Butch Cassidy and the Sundance Kid
      Robert Redford   *Robert Conrad*   *Robert Vaughn*

On the Road

The automobile is part and parcel of almost every American's life. You may spend a good portion of your day in one of these horseless carriages — but how much do you really know about them?

Below you will find 28 questions on the automobile. You are given four choices for each. Check the one you think is correct.

Give yourself three points for each correct answer. Deduct one point for each incorrect answer. A score below 25 marks you as pedestrian; 44 puts you in the driver's seat; 60 makes you every passenger's favorite. If you score a perfect 84, well, you're a real hot rod!

1. The first truly practical gasoline-powered auto was the French Panhard, designed in:

   1885 *1889* *1894* *1899*

2. In 1898, the number of automobile manufacturers was:

   5 *10* *25* *50*

3. In 1923, a Ford Model T sold for:

   $295 *$495* *$895* *$1295*

4. The first man to travel 300 m.p.h. in a car was:

   Gary Gabelich *Craig Breedlove*
   Malcolm Campbell *Mario Andretti*

5. The first President to ride in an automobile was:

   McKinley *T. Roosevelt* *Taft* *Wilson*

6. The most popular American car is (according to 1971 figures):

   Chevrolet *Ford* *Oldsmobile* *Cadillac*

7. The most reckless drivers in the world, with 31.9 traffic deaths per 100,000 population are in:

   Italy *France* *U.S.A.* *Austria*

8. The first automobile race ever held was won by a steam-powered car which traveled 80 miles at a rate of:

   7 m.p.h. *17 m.p.h.* *27 m.p.h.* *37 m.p.h.*

180

9. The first man to win the Indianapolis 500 was:
   Henry Ford   *Gaston Chevrolet*   *Tommy Milton*   *Lou Mezer*

10. In its heyday, Ford's flivver sold for about:
    $250   *$300*   *$400*   *$500*

11. The largest car ever produced for private use was the 1927 "Golden Bugatti." Its length was:
    18 feet   *20 feet*   *22 feet*   *24 feet*

12. Of the following autos, the only one still being produced is the:
    Corvair   *Hudson*   *Studebaker*   *Lincoln*

13. The inventor of the rotary engine was:
    Duryea   *Wankel*   *Stutz*   *Mazda*

14. Of the following, the car which depreciates least in trade-in value is the:
    Chevrolet   *Ford*   *Volkswagen*   *Cadillac*

15. The Saab is made in:
    Denmark   *Norway*   *Sweden*   *Finland*

16. The French city noted for its automobile races is:
    Monza   *Le Mans*   *Sebring*   *Cannes*

17. The first car to be manufactured in Detroit was made in:
    1887   *1892*   *1896*   *1900*

18. The man generally conceded to have built the first self-propelled automobile was:
    Nicholas Cugnot   *Karl Benz*   *Charles Duryea*   *Henry Ford*

19. All of the following items increase gas consumption except:
    Radial tires   *Automatic transmission*
    Air conditioning   *Emission control devices*

20. The auto instrument which shows the number of wheel revolutions per minute is called the:
    Odometer   *Speedometer*   *Tachometer*   *Rheometer*

21. Of the following autos, the only one that is *not* manufactured in Japan is the:
    Datsun   *Volvo*   *Mazda*   *Toyota*

181

TV Teasers

Are you a TV maven? Below are 45 statements about the tube. Each contains a blank. Fill in the word or phrase that will complete the sentence.

A score of 25 is fair; 30 is a good show; 40 is a stellar performance.

1. The longest-running Western in television history is

   _____.

2. In *Dragnet,* Sergeant Joe Friday worked for the police department in

   the city of _____.

3. The first commercial TV broadcast in the United States took place in

   the year _____.

4. Dobie Gillis' beatnik friend was named _____.

5. The host of *The Show of Shows* was _____.

6. Of the three major networks, the one with the most affiliates is

   _____.

7. A late '50s variety show starring Edie Adams and her husband was

   _____.

8. The star of *Highway Patrol* was _____.

9. In *The Fugitive,* Richard Kimble was accused of killing

   _____.

10. On *The Donna Reed Show,* Donna's husband, Dr. Stone, was played

    by _____.

11. In *Bonanza,* the Cartwright ranch was called _____.

12. The hero of *Have Gun, Will Travel* was known as

    _____.

13. The Cisco Kid's sidekick was called _____.

14. The name of the clown on *The Howdy Doody Show* was

    _____.

15. The name of Abbott and Costello's landlord was

    _____.

16. Patty Duke's little brother Ross was played by _____.

17. *Naked City* was set in _____.

18. Topper was played by _____.

19. The Lone Ranger's horse was named _____.

20. The name of Perry Mason's secretary was _____.

21. *The FBI* starred _____.

22. Flash Gordon was played by _____.

23. Olympic star Johnny Weissmuller starred in a show called

    _____.

24. In *Amos and Andy*, the name of Kingfish's wife was

    _____.

25. *The Mary Tyler Moore Show* was set in _____.

26. On *The Andy Griffith Show*, Don Knotts played a deputy named

    _____.

27. Davy Crockett was played by _____.

28. Since 1955 Bob Keeshan has been playing _____.

29. In *Disneyland*, the four kingdoms were *Frontierland, Tomorrowland,*

    Adventureland, and _____.

30. The name of TV's annual awards is the _____.

31. `The name of Fred Flintstone's wife was _____.

32. In *The Honeymooners*, Ralph Cramden worked as a

   _____.

33. The captain of the P.T. boat in *McHale's Navy* was played by

   _____.

34. In *The Man from U.C.L.E.*, Robert Vaughn played the character

   _____.

35. The single program watched by more people than any other was

   _____.

36. The hero of *The Untouchables* was _____.

37. The creator and host of the *Twilight Zone* series was

   _____.

38. Jim Nabors played the role of a Marine named _____.

39. In *All in the Family*, the name of Archie Bunker's wife is

   _____.

40. Carol Burnett's leading man for 10 seasons was _____.

41. E.G. Marshall and Robert Reed played father and son in a
   courtroom drama series entitled _____.

42. The original *Laugh-In* was hosted by _____.

43. The title character in *Phyllis* was played by _____.

44. What character did Ron Howard of *Happy Days* play on the old
   Andy Griffith Show? _____.

45. *Maude* and *The Jeffersons* are spin-offs from _____.

Are You Decisive?

The inclination to make decisions on the spur of the moment is a handicap in many walks of life, and is fatal in some. Yet there are occasions when spot decisions must be made, though we would rather suspend judgment; when indecision is worse than a wrong decision.

This challenging test deals with only one of the many "quick decision" situations encountered in life, many of which involve factors completely different from those significant here. Yet the tasks that follow do indicate whether you can act with more or less decisiveness and accuracy than others under like circumstances.

Give yourself one point for each answer. A score of below 6 is poor; 6–8, is fair; 9–11, good; over 11 superior; and 14 is perfect.

PART ONE

DIRECTIONS: In each of the following groups of figures, decide which three rows in each group add up to the three largest sums, and place a check next to these rows. You will not have time to actually add all the rows; you must make the best guess you can. TIME LIMIT: 1 MINUTE

Group 1:

_____ A. 1234567

_____ B. 1123458

_____ C. 7654321

_____ D. 2375686

_____ E. 2345667

_____ F. 1117771

_____ G. 2834568

_____ H. 2113458

Group 2:

_____ A. 1111555

_____ B. 1515151

_____ C. 1646515

_____ D. 5646011

_____ E. 6115540

_____ F. 1205641

_____ G. 1536751

_____ H. 1733165

Group 3:

_____ A. 1579832

_____ B. 9036721

_____ C. 8895361

_____ D. 4564539

_____ E. 6932199

_____ F. 5412838

_____ G. 1988756

_____ H. 5676587

PART TWO

DIRECTIONS: Below are nine rows of letters. Decide which three rows contain the most letters, and place a check next to these rows. You will not have time to actually count the letters, so guess as shrewdly as you can. TIME LIMIT: 15 SECONDS

_____ 1. BBBBB BBBBB BBBBB

_____ 2. BWBWBWB BWBWBWB

_____ 3. WWWWWW WWWWWW

_____ 4. OOOOO OOOOOO OOOOO

_____ 5. IIIIIII IIIIII IIIIII IIIIIII

_____ 6. VOVOVOVOVOVO VOVOVOVO

_____ 7. IIIIII IIIII IIIIII IIIII IIIIII

_____ 8. WIWIWIWIWIWIWIW

_____ 9. VIII VIIII VIIII VIII VIIII VIII

186

PART THREE

DIRECTIONS: Each circle below is divided into sections. Check the two circles which are divided into the greatest number of sections. You will not have time to count the sections, so guess as shrewdly as you can. TIME LIMIT: 15 SECONDS

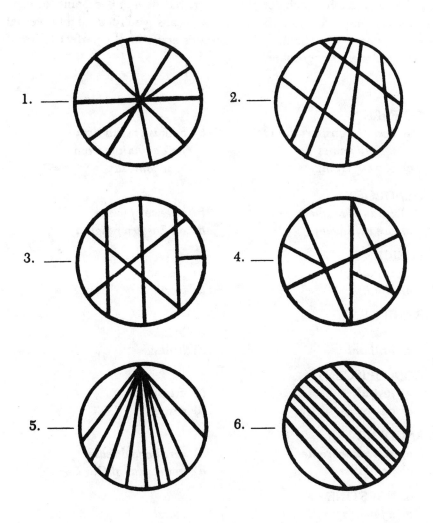

1. ———

2. ———

3. ———

4. ———

5. ———

6. ———

Vocabulary Quiz II

You have undoubtedly encountered these 29 words in newspapers, magazines and books. You probably know approximately what they mean; but do you exactly know what they mean?

Mark the choice you believe to be correct. Check your answers; give yourself two points for each correct answer, but deduct one point for each incorrect response. A total score of 32 means you're a highly verbal person; 40 means you should join Webster's staff; and a perfect score of 58 means you're a lexicographer.

1. FANFARE
   a) cost of transportation to ball games
   c) blast of trumpets
   b) Spanish menu item
   d) fee deductible from income tax

2. OENOLOGY
   a) study of seashells
   c) ocean biology
   b) science of wines
   d) an Eastern religion

3. PUERILE
   a) valuable
   c) childish
   b) enamel
   d) sterile

4. EFFULGENT
   a) brassy
   c) brilliant
   b) brittle
   d) bruised

5. CONCUPISCENT
   a) lustful
   c) clever
   b) attractive
   d) costly

6. ANODYNE
   a) mercurochrome
   c) painkiller
   b) rare bone disease
   d) in the year of Our Lord

7. CLANDESTINE
   a) a famous family
   c) musical instrument
   b) secret
   d) brightly colored

8. DONNYBROOK
    a) brawl
    b) large farm
    c) small stream
    d) Scottish national bird

9. GOSSAMER
    a) young goose
    b) gaseous
    c) gauzy
    d) bitter-tasting

10. TRENCHANT
    a) foxhole
    b) incisive
    c) ditchdigger
    d) wooden platter

11. ENCOMIUM
    a) praise
    b) prison
    c) prize
    d) price

12. WINSOME
    a) victorious
    b) lucky
    c) unappealing
    d) charming

13. EPITOME
    a) circumference
    b) essence
    c) grandeur
    d) large book

14. RECIDIVIST
    a) democrat
    b) habitual criminal
    c) socialist
    d) front-desk secretary

15. CRASS
    a) unfeeling
    b) salad green
    c) synthetic metal
    d) emotional

16. GAFFE
    a) desert animal
    b) lady's hat
    c) blunder
    d) nonsense

17. PARIAH
    a) outcast
    b) outhouse
    c) outdoors
    d) outlandish

18. VICARIOUS
    a) clerical
    b) funny
    c) dangerous
    d) substitute

19. INCONOCLASTIC
    a) durable plastic
    c) strong elastic
    b) traditional
    d) revolutionary

20. NADIR
    a) lowest point
    c) poor
    b) government official
    d) Hindu garment

21. DEPREDATE
    a) plunder
    c) intercede
    b) belittle
    d) precede

22. MAUDLIN
    a) ordinary
    c) stately
    b) purple
    d) sentimental

23. MILITATE
    a) march
    c) have effect
    b) lessen
    d) conscript

24. RESCIND
    a) sin again
    c) rekindle
    b) revoke
    d) tough rind

25. PEREGRINATION
    a) journey
    c) puzzle
    b) dove-like
    d) disease

26. SUBSIST
    a) be a category of
    c) hang up
    b) continue to exist
    d) flood with water

27. INTERLOPER
    a) dramatist
    c) aviator
    b) conversationalist
    d) intruder

28. HARBINGER
    a) omen
    c) gambler
    b) magician
    d) type of horse

29. DIFFIDENCE
    a) shyness
    c) distinction
    b) trust
    d) stubbornness

190

Do You Know Kids?

Read each statement and decide whether you think it is True or False. Give yourself two points for each correct response; but deduct one point for each incorrect answer. A score of 7 makes you a desirable baby sitter; 14 entitles you to work in a nursery program; and with a perfect score of 20 you can join the Harvard research team.

1. Real intelligence and learning do not begin until the child is about six, which is why school usually begins at this age. T F

2. The cooing and babbling that babies engage in are meaningless. T F

3. The receptive vocabulary (words that are understood) of a six-year-old who has been raised in a family that talks and reads to him is between 15,000 and 25,000 words. T F

4. Small children are best kept in playpens where they can concentrate on one or two toys at a time. T F

5. Children's questions should be answered as seriously and correctly as possible, regardless of how silly or complex they may be. T F

6. A parent or baby sitter should not attempt to teach a child to read before the youngster has the guidance of a trained teacher. T F

7. Small children learn primarily through the sense of sight. T F

8. Children who are always "getting into things" are naughty and should be curbed because of the danger of accidents or disease. T F

9. Small children should be shown the correct way to play with each of their toys. T F

10. Small children should seldom, if ever, be taken on shopping trips with parents. T F

Presidential Precedents

Every American girl and boy can grow up to be President, but only 38 have so far. How much do you know about these heads of our country?

Score one point for every answer you got right. A total score of 15 is not so bad; 20 means you have a good head for history; and anything over 25 marks you as likely candidate for the Cabinet, at least; a perfect score is 31, but then you'd rather be right than president.

1. Who was the first Democrat to be elected President of the United States, and when was he elected?
   a. George Washington   b. Martin Van Buren
   c. Thomas Jefferson   d. Andrew Jackson
   e. 1836   f. 1800   g. 1828   h. 1789

2. Which President had the largest family?
   a. T. Roosevelt   b. W.H. Harrison   c. J. Tyler   d. F.D. Roosevelt

3. Which President had the longest life span?
   a. Hoover   b. Jefferson   c. Truman   d. Madison

4. Four of our State Capitals were named for four of our Presidents. Can you name them?
   a. _____   b. _____
   c. _____   d. _____

5. Four of our Presidents died in office from natural causes. Can you name them?
   a. _____   b. _____
   c. _____   d. _____

6. Four of our Presidents were assassinated in office. Can you name them?
   a. _____   b. _____
   c. _____   d. _____

7. Which President was born on July 4th?
   a. Grant   b. Coolidge   c. Eisenhower   d. Taft

8. Two Presidents died on July 4th; as a matter of fact, both of them in the same year. Can you name them?

   a. _____   b. _____

9. Who was the tallest President?

   a. *Andrew Jackson*   b. *Thomas Jefferson*
   c. *Lyndon Johnson*   d. *Abraham Lincoln*

   and the shortest?

   e. *John Adams*   f. *Hayes*
   g. *Madison*   h. *Benjamin Harrison*

10. One American woman was the wife of one of our Presidents and the mother of another. Who was she?

   a. *Abigail Smith*   b. *Grace Goodhue*
   c. *Rose Fitzgerald*   d. *Sarah Delano*

11. Who was the first President to be the subject of a serious drive for impeachment?

   a. *Polk*   b. *Van Buren*   c. *Nixon*   d. *Tyler*

12. Franklin D. Roosevelt was elected to the Presidency four consecutive times. Who was his Republican opponent each time?

   a. *In 1932* _____   b. *1936* _____
   c. *1940* _____   d. *1944* _____

13. Which President was an excellent tailor and made most of his own clothes?

   a. *John Quincy Adams*   b. *Zachary Taylor*
   c. *Andrew Johnson*   d. *James Buchanan*

14. Who was President when the cotton gin was invented?

   a. *Lincoln*   b. *Jefferson*   c. *Madison*   d. *Washington*

15. Who was President when the 18th (Prohibition) Amendment became law?

   a. *T. Roosevelt*   b. *Harding*   c. *Wilson*   d. *McKinley*

16. Who was President when the 21st Amendment (repealing prohibition) became law?

   a. *Coolidge*   b. *Hoover*   c. *F.D. Roosevelt*   d. *Truman*

Grab Bag

Here's a test of your general knowledge of inconsequential facts. Now you can find out how much tangential mental junk you have accumulated over a lifetime.

Mark the answer you think is correct. Then check yourself. Score one point for each correct answer. A score of 10 is fair; 15 is good; 20 exceptional; and 22 is supercallifragilisticexpialidosious!

1. The largest country in South America is:
    a) Chile   b) Argentina   c) Peru   d) Brazil

2. Pat Nixon's real name is:
    a) Mamie   b) Thelma   c) Josephine   d) Jacqueline

3. The author of "The Idylls of the King" was the poet:
    a) Edmund Spenser   b) Thomas Malory
    c) Alfred Tennyson   d) Robert Browning

4. In Greek mythology, the god of the ocean was:
    a) Poseidon   b) Zeus   c) Apollo   d) Hephaestus

5. The star of the T.V. show "The Fugitive" was:
    a) Warren Beatty   b) Ben Gazarra
    c) David Janssen   d) Efram Zimbalist, Jr.

6. A Reuben sandwich consists of:
    a) Pastrami and mustard   b) Bacon, lettuce, and tomato
    c) Turkey and ham   d) Corned beef and swiss cheese

7. Mother's Day became an official holiday in:
    a) 1914   b) 1814   c) 1776   d) 1900

8. In the U. S., artichokes grow primarily in:
    a) Texas   b) California   c) Vermont   d) Indiana

9. The Dionnes are famous as:
    a) Acrobats   b) Quintuplets   c) Singers   d) Psychics

194

10. The 1970 Kentucky Derby winner was:
    a) *Dust Commander*   b) *Personality*
    c) *Dancer's Image*   d) *Candy Spots*

11. The age of the radio soap opera heroine Helen Trent was:
    a) *19*   b) *29*   c) *39*   d) *49*

12. The total land area of Alabama is approximately:
    a) *5,000 square miles*   b) *50,000 square miles*
    c) *500,000 square miles*   d) *150,000 square miles*

13. A licorice-tasting herb is:
    a) *Cardamom*   b) *Fennel*   c) *Sage*   d) *Thyme*

14. The dish called *pommes soufflés* consists of:
    a) *Potatoes*   b) *Apples*   c) *Cheese*   d) *Egg whites*

15. The Kodak Camera was invented by:
    a) *Joseph Niepce*   b) *Louis Daguerre*
    c) *George Eastman*   d) *Thomas Edison*

16. The capital of the state of Washington is:
    a) *Tacoma*   b) *Olympia*   c) *Seattle*   d) *Spokane*

17. Alexander Fleming, the inventor of penicillin, won the Nobel Prize in:
    a) *1895*   b) *1945*   c) *1905*   d) *1970*

18. The number of players on a cricket team is:
    a) *9*   b) *11*   c) *5*   d) *14*

19. Athlete Kareem Abdul-Jabbar was once known as:
    a) *Cassius Clay*   b) *Lew Alcindor*
    c) *Wilt Chamberlain*   d) *Walt Bellamy*

20. The 18th President of the United States was:
    a) *Millard Fillmore*   b) *Ulysses S. Grant*
    c) *Theodore Roosevelt*   d) *Abraham Lincoln*

21. Peach Melba is the name of:
    a) *An opera star*   b) *A baseball player*   c) *A dessert*   d) *A color*

22. The 1965 Academy Award for best actress went to Julie Christie for:
    a) *Petulia*   b) *Darling*   c) *Shampoo*   d) *Dr. Zhivago*

Are You Well-Read?

Below are 25 questions that will test your literary expertise. Mark the answer you believe is correct.

A score of 13 is good; 19 is superior; and 22 marks you as a librarian.

1. The fair Desdemona is the victim of Iago's perfidy in:
   Macbeth   *Othello*
   King Lear   *Hamlet*

2. Of the following novels, the one *not* written by Sir Walter Scott is:
   Ivanhoe   *Kenilworth*
   The Heart of Midlothian   *Lorna Doone*

3. A Civil War general named Lew Wallace was the author of:
   Stillness at Appomattox   *Little Women*
   Ben-Hur   *An American Tragedy*

4. Fyodor Dostoevski's character Raskolnikov appears in the novel:
   Crime and Punishment   *The Possessed*
   The Brothers Karamazov   *The Idiot*

5. Norman Mailer's first novel was:
   American Dream   *The Naked and the Dead*
   Barbary Shore   *The Deer Park*

6. *The Wasteland* is a celebrated long poem by:
   Ezra Pound   *Robert Lowell*
   W. B. Yeats   *T. S. Eliot*

7. Huckleberry Finn's compatriot on the raft was a slave named:
   Joe   *Jim*
   John   *Jed*

8. Thomas Hardy gave up novel-writing at the height of his career because of the unfavorable reaction to:
   The Mayor of Casterbridge *The Return of the Native*
   Tess of the D'Urbervilles *Jude the Obscure*

9. Sir Arthur Conan Doyle's Sherlock Holmes lived at:
   10 Downing Street   *22 Downing Street*
   22 Baker Street   *10 Baker Street*

10. The protagonist of Victor Hugo's *Les Miserables* was named:
    Maurice Richard   *Jean Javert*
    George Feydean   *Jean Valjean*

11. Of the following novels, the one *not* written by James Joyce is:
    Finnegan's Wake   *Ulysses*
    Orlando   *Portrait of the Artist as a Young Man*

12. The term "girl Friday" can be traced back to the novel:
    Clarissa Harlowe   *Robinson Crusoe*
    Emma   *Swiss Family Robinson*

13. The first "detective story" in the English language was *The Moonstone*, written by:
    William Wilkie Collins   *Erle Stanley Gardner*
    Arthur Conan Doyle   *James Branch Cabell*

14. *The Invisible Man* was written by H.G. Wells. A quite different book, called *Invisible Man*, is the work of:
    Ray Bradbury   *Ralph Ellison*
    John Updike   *Gore Vidal*

15. Vladimir Nabokov did *not* write:
    Lolita   *Nana*   *Pale Fire*   *Ada*

16. The playwright of *Peter Pan* was:
    Harold Pinter   *James Barrie*
    Mary Martin   *George Bernard Shaw*

17. Dante's *Divine Comedy* is divided into:
    2 parts   *6 parts*
    3 parts   *10 parts*

18. Henrik Ibsen was *not* the author of:
    Miss Julie   *Peer Gynt*
    A Doll's House   *The Wild Duck*

In Other Words

If you want to see the unholy effect of clothing a simple thought with bombastic verbosity, slant your gaze at the following sentences. Hidden away beneath the lush overgrowth of phrases are some plain, simple ideas which you know as common maxims. Can you penetrate the verbiage and extricate the proverbs?

If you can unravel 9 of them, you needn't be blue. If you score 12, you deserve a blue pencil. If you deliver them all, you deserve a blue ribbon.

1. A mass of concreted earthy material perennially rotating on its axis will not accumulate an accretion of byrophytic vegetation.

2. A superabundance of talent skilled in the preparation of gastronomic concoctions will impair the quality of a certain potable solution made by immersing a gallinaceous bird in ebullient Adam's ale.

3. Individuals who perforce are constrained to be domiciled in vitreous structures of patent frangibility should on no account employ petrous formations as projectiles.

4. The prudent avis which matutinally deserts the coziness of its abode will ensnare a vermiculate creature.

5. Everything that coruscates with effulgence is not ipso facto aurous.

6. Do not dissipate your competence by hebetudinous prodigality lest you subsequently lament an exigent inadequacy.

7. An addle-pated beetlehead and his specie divaricate with startling prematurity.

8. It can be no other than a maleficent propelled current of gaseous matter whose portentous advent is not the harbinger of a modicum of beneficence.

_____

9. One should hyperesthetically exercise macrography upon that situs which one will eventually tenant if one propels oneself into the troposphere.

_____

10. Aberration is the hallmark of homo sapiens; while longanimous placability and condonation are the indicia of supramundane omni-science.

_____

11. It is a futile undertaking to lament the evacuation from a container of bovine nutrient matter.

_____

12. The circular disc revolving on its axis with short, shrill sounds is wont to receive an application of unguentary matter.

_____

13. One is able to make a greater number of Dipterae captive by employing sweet viscid nectar than by employing acetic acid.

_____

14. There is a dearth of oaves exhibiting a similarity to superannuated oaves.

_____

15. One is at a distinct disadvantage attempting to educate an aging hound in recent prestidigitation.

_____

16. A large round earthenware vessel subject to the observation of a plethora of persons on no occasion reaches a temperature of 100 degrees Centigrade.

_____

Checklist for the Literati

Here is a list of expressions which don't literally mean what they say. You've probably run across all of them as you've turned the pages of literature. If you're up on your literary allusions—both classic and common—most of these 22 phrases should be in the bag!

A score of 17 will be a feather in your cap, while an achievement of 19 should transport you to seventh heaven!

1. To Kick the Bucket
   To defy one's superiors
   To flunk out of West Point
   To depart this life

2. Between Scylla and Charybdis
   To be torn between two loves
   Between two dangers, neither of which can be avoided
   Loss of both money and honor

3. To Turn the Cat in the Pan
   To cleverly give a dexterous turn to a situation
   To accuse one's accuser
   To accomplish a miracle

4. A White Elephant
   A burdensome possession
   An institution that exists only through lavish endowments
   A profitless business maintained solely through sentiment

5. To Cry Wolf
   To give alarm without occasion
   To frighten by a ruse
   To claim aggression while one attacks

6. A Barmecide Feast
   An easy piece of change
   An illusion of plenty
   An orgy of gluttony

7. To Talk Like a Dutch Uncle

   To admonish with severity and directness
   To insist
   To make lavish promises

8. Sour Grapes

   Cut-throat competition
   Things affectedly despised because they cannot be possessed
   A secret cause of hidden irritation

9. To Walk in Golden Slippers

   To be rolling in riches
   To dream or imagine that one is wealthy
   To belong to a clerical order

10. Attic Salt

    Poignant, delicate wit
    Money used for bribes
    Sarcasm

11. To Cut the Gordian Knot

    To dispose of a difficulty by prompt, arbitrary action
    To break into a society where one has been spurned
    To act snobbishly

12. A Simon Legree

    A cruel taskmaster
    A mean old miser
    A fiendish experience

13. To Tilt at Windmills

    To petition the government
    To fight imaginary enemies
    To attempt the useless

14. A Mare's Nest

    An absurd belief
    A quest that is beyond attainment
    An undiscovered love

15. Dining with Duke Humphrey
    To be invited by relatives
    To act snobbishly
    To go without dinner

16. Born to the Purple
    Of imperial birth
    Congenitally angry
    Born both rich and handsome

17. To Play Ducks and Drakes
    To placate both parties in a controversy
    To squander foolishly
    To vacillate and waste time

18. Waving the Bloody Shirt
    Stirring up or reviving sectional animosity
    Demanding ransom under threat
    To signal for peace

19. A Pyrrhic Victory
    A victory gained at too great cost
    A complete rout
    A military triumph

20. To Sow Dragon's Teeth
    To bring up children with hatred
    To count on a future success which is beyond hope
    To follow policies which will lead to war

21. A Fabian Policy
    Dilatory tactics calculated to wear out the enemy
    Outward conciliation while secretly arming
    Flattery

22. A Pig in a Poke
    A quick mind
    Something whose true value is unknown
    A great bargain

202

Quiet on the Set!

You've probably heard of all these films, and you may even have seen all of them, but can you identify their directors? See how many of the following movies and directors you can match.

A score of 22 indicates you know your cinema; 29 makes you a real movie buff; 35 means you should have been a film critic!

1. *The Seventh Seal*
   Ingmar Bergman   George Cukor   Henri Costa-Gavras

2. *Gone with the Wind*
   Cecil B. DeMille   D.W. Griffith   Victor Fleming

3. *Nashville*
   Robert Altman   Bob Fosse   Roman Polanski

4. *Seven Beauties*
   Jeanne Moreau   Agnes Varda   Lina Wertmuller

5. *Psycho*
   Orson Welles   Sydney Pollack   Alfred Hitchcock

6. *La Dolce Vita*
   Federico Fellini   Ettore Scola   Michelangelo Antonioni

7. *Sleeper*
   Mel Brooks   Robert Altman   Woody Allen

8. *The Last Picture Show*
   Peter Bogdanovich   John Schlesinger   Bryan de Palma

9. *Romeo and Juliet*
   Roberto Rosselini   Paolo Tavioni   Franco Zeffirelli

10. *One Flew Over the Cuckoo's Nest*
    Edward L. Kahn   Milos Forman   Peter Yates

11. *Some Like It Hot*
    Mack Sennett   Billy Wilder   Luchino Visconti

12. *The Sting*
    Paul Newman   George Roy Hill   George Lucas

13. *Holiday*
    George Kuchar   George Cukor   Joan Darling

14. *Harold and Maude*
    John Frankenheimer   Hal Ashby   Elia Kazan

15. *Women in Love*
    Edward L. Kahn   Ken Russell   David Lean

16. *Mr. Deeds Goes to Town*
    Preston Sturges   Charles Vidor   Frank Capra

17. *Bringing Up Baby*
    Charles Vidor   Frank Capra   Howard Hawks

18. *The Go-Between*
    Ben Hecht   Joseph Losey   Charles Barton

19. *Hang 'Em High*
    John Ford   Sergio Leone   John Huston

20. *Birth of a Nation*
    Erich von Stroheim   D.W. Griffith   Stanley Donen

21. *Long Day's Journey into Night*
    George Lucas   Lamont Jonhson   Sidney Lumet

22. *Star Wars*
    George Roy Hill   Stanley Kubrick   George Lucas

23. *Henry V*
    Sir John Gielgud   Paul Scofield   Laurence Olivier

24. *Citizen Kane*
    Orson Welles   Stanley Kubrick   Raoul Walsh

25. *The Ten Commandments*
    Cecil B. DeMille   Robert Leonard   David O. Selznick

26. *Casablanca*
    Fred Zinnemann   Michael Curtiz   Robert Rossen

27. *All About Eve*
    Vincente Minnelli   Paul Lynch   Joseph Mankiewicz

28. *Z*
    Andy Warhol   Henri Costa-Gavras   Jean-Luc Godard

29. *The Sound of Music*
    Robert Wise   Michael Lean   Jerome Robbins

30. *Close Encounters of the Third Kind*
    Martin Ritt   Stephen Spielberg   George Pal

31. *The Exorcist*
    Stanley Kramer   Alfred Hitchcock   William Friedkin

32. *M*
    Alfred Hitchcock   Fritz Lang   King Vidor

33. *The Decameron*
    Renato Castellani   Francesco Rossi   Pier Paolo Pasolini

34. *Gentlemen Prefer Blondes*
    Flo Ziegfeld   George Cukor   Howard Hawks

35. *Taxi Driver*
    Robert Altman   Martin Scorcese   Nicholas Roeg

36. *Dr. Strangelove*
    Andy Warhol   Stanley Kubrick   Stanley Donen

37. *Jaws*
    Stephen Spielberg   George Lucas   William Friedkin

38. *Rebel Without a Cause*
    Nicholas Ray   Walter Hill   Robert Aldrich

39. *The Wizard of Oz*
    George Cukor   Victor Fleming   Cecil B. DeMille

40. *The French Connection*
    Peter Bogdanovich   William Friedkin   Walter Hill

Do You Know Food?

America is famous for ethnic restaurants of every nationality. Would you like to test your international culinary skills with the following 27 questions?

Fifteen right answers show an adventurous palate; 20 label you as a gourmet; 25 or more mark you as a gastronome *par excellence*.

1. Pasta, layered with tomato sauce, cheese and (sometimes) meat, composes:

   Lasagna   *Cassoulet*
   Pasta con brodo   *Cous-cous*

2. The Brazilian native dish of world renown is:

   Tortillas   *Chili con carne*
   Feijoada completa   *Paella*

3. A key ingredient of a Caesar salad is:

   Coddled egg   Bacon
   Fruit   Potatoes

4. *Sashimi*, that Nipponese delicacy, is nothing more or less than:

   Broiled lobster   Japanese beef stew
   Raw fish   Spicy pickled cabbage

5. *Fettucine verdi* is Italian for:

   Potato dumplings   Green noodles
   Saffron rice   Rice and beans

6. Szechuan cuisine, now coming into vogue all over the world, is characterized by:

   Blandness   Delicacy
   Spiciness   Sweetness

7. *A la mode* means:

   With whipped cream   Piping hot
   With ice cream   Without sauce

8. *Bratwurst,* so popular at Oktoberfests, is:

   Kosher pickle

   Austrian ham

   German salami

   Pork sausage

9. *Crèpes Suzette,* delectable to the palate, are:

   Omelettes

   Dessert pancakes

   Shrimp hors-d'oeuvres

   Marinated stringbeans

10. A delicious Indian soup is called:

    Minestrone

    Mulligatawny

    Egg drop

    Vichysoisse

11. *Empañadas* is the Spanish name for:

    Meat pies

    Fruit pies

    Cream pies

    Meringue pies

12. Stuffed grape leaves, beloved throughout Greece and the Middle East, are:

    Dolmadas

    Moussaka

    Mestizo

    Baklava

13. Sour cream is a key ingredient in:

    Beef stroganoff

    Mussels *marinierès*

    Shrimp cocktail

    Trout *meuniere*

14. The Indonesian version of the smorgasboard is called:

    Rissole

    Humus

    Rijsttafel

    Burrito

15. *Cuisine minceur,* the hot new item among French gourmet chefs, means:

    Fried in butter

    Low calorie

    Extra spicy

    Finely minced

16. Hungarian stew is known as:

    Daube

    Casserole

    Goulash

    Zuppa

17. *Flambé* means:

    Doused in cognac and ignited

    Extravagant

    Fried quickly

    Ice cream dessert

Commander-in-Chief

Can you answer the following 20 multiple-choice questions on past American presidents?

A score of 10 makes you a good citizen; 15 means you are a history buff; 18 means you may have presidential aspirations yourself!

1. What early president served as a member of the House of Representatives after his term as president?
    John Quincy Adams   *John Adams*   *Thomas Jefferson*

2. Which president said, "Speak softly and carry a big stick."
    Teddy Roosevelt   *Franklin D. Roosevelt*   *Herbert Hoover*

3. Who said, "We have nothing to fear but fear itself."
    Woodrow Wilson   *Franklin D. Roosevelt*   *Harry S. Truman*

4. Which president said, "Prosperity is just around the corner."
    Andrew Johnson   *Franklin D. Roosevelt*   *Herbert Hoover*

5. Two former presidents died on July 4, 1826. One was John Adams; who was the other?
    Thomas Jefferson   *James Madison*   *George Washington*

6. Who was the first vice-president to resign his office?
    John C. Calhoun   *John C. Breckinridge*   *Spiro Agnew*

7. What Democratic vice-presidential candidate in 1920 was later elected president?
    Franklin D. Roosevelt   *Harry S. Truman*   *Calvin Coolidge*

8. Which president was Chief Justice after having been president?
    Martin Van Buren   *Chester A. Arthur*   *William Howard Taft*

9. Who was the first president to die in office?
    Andrew Jackson   *William Henry Harrison*   *Abraham Lincoln*

10. Even though Aaron Burr is famous for having killed Alexander Hamilton in a duel, the truth is that one of our presidents also emerged victorious after a duel. Which one?
    John Quincy Adams   *Zachary Taylor*   *Andrew Jackson*

11. Who was the first president elected after women were given the vote?

    Calvin Coolidge   *Warren G. Harding*   *Teddy Roosevelt*

12. A tragic coincidence, going far back in our history, is that every president elected in a year ending in zero has died in office. With what election year did this chain begin?

    1820   *1840*   *1860*

13. What president was in residence at the White House when it was burned by the British?

    James Madison   *James Monroe*   *Thomas Jefferson*

14. Who was the youngest man ever sworn in as president?

    Teddy Roosevelt   *John Quincy Adams*   *John F. Kennedy*

15. How many presidents have died by assassination?

    3   *4*   *15*

16. Which president's term was marred by the Teapot Dome scandal?

    Ulysses S. Grant   *Warren G. Harding*   *Calvin Coolidge*

17. Which of the following old American political parties never elected a man to the White House?

    Whigs   *Federalists*   *Populists*

18. Which was the last president to welcome a new state into the union?

    Harry S. Truman   *Dwight D. Eisenhower*   *John F. Kennedy*

19. What 20th-century president married while in office?

    Calvin Coolidge   *Franklin D. Roosevelt*   *Woodrow Wilson*

20. What state has produced eight presidents—more than any other?

    Virginia   *New York*   *Massachusetts*

How to Solve Cryptograms

To some people a cryptogram is nothing more nor less than one of the milder forms of self-torture; but a lot of people think cryptograms are a lot of fun. If you thrill to tales of espionage and fantasize yourself a secret agent, you will find decoding cryptograms a fascinating pastime.

A cryptogram is a secret message in which one letter has been systematically substituted for another letter. To break the code, you have to figure out what each letter in the message really stands for.

This might seem altogether arbitrary and virtually impossible. But not so. Linguists have come up with information about the English language that is very helpful to cryptographers. They tell us, for example, that all English words include one or more vowels, and that the five vowels—A, E, I, O, U—comprise 40 percent of all written communications. The letters L, N, R, S, and T comprise 30 percent of usage; and J, K, Q, X, and Z comprise but 2 percent. The remaining 11 letters comprise 28 percent of words commonly used in written English.

Armed with this information, you are ready to tackle any cryptogram. You might want to write each letter of the alphabet, followed by an equal sign, on a piece of paper. One-letter words are, of course, likely to be "I" or "A." Examine the coded message to see how often each letter appears. It is a good hypothesis that the letter which appears most often stands for E. Examine especially the three-letter words. If the same three-letter combination appears frequently, and the third letter is also the letter that appears most frequently throughout, the chances are the word is THE. For example, if A B Z appears four or five times, and Z appears most frequently throughout, it is a fairly safe bet that A B Z stands for THE. Write T under A wherever it appears in the message; H under B; and E under Z.

Now examine the coded words again. If there are any two-letter words beginning with A standing for T, the chances are the word is TO. Continue making educated guesses, changing your hypotheses whenever that becomes necessary, until you break the code.

Don't forget to time yourself. If you are a novice in cryptography, you're doing well to solve the cryptogram in Par Time. As you become more proficient, aim for a Medal Score.

Pratfall

PAR: 25 minutes   MEDAL SCORE: 17 minutes

Q P Y Y B D T   O E   B   E R   X F T I J F N S I
_ _ _ _ _ _ _   _ _   _   _ _   _ _ _ _ _ _ _ _ _

N F W E Y J;   R E   Y B   I S   J E   Q T   G E J J E Q
_ _ _ _ _ _   _ _   _ _ _ _   _ _   _ _   _ _ _ _ _ _

B R   J X B I   S B R O   E V   I H E Y J.
_ _   _ _ _ _   _ _ _ _   _ _   _ _ _ _ _

Headstrong

PAR: 25 minutes   MEDAL SCORE: 15 minutes

Y C P   B N M J   N H   N Y H   G V M   U I F S P,
_ _ _   _ _ _ _   _ _   _ _ _   _ _ _   _ _ _ _ _

F M J   N M   N Y H P I E   S F M   B F X P
_ _ _   _ _   _ _ _ _ _ _   _ _ _   _ _ _ _

F   C P F A P M   G E   C P I I,   F
_   _ _ _ _ _ _   _ _   _ _ _ _   _

C P I I   G E   C P F A P M.
_ _ _ _   _ _   _ _ _ _ _ _

Farewell, False Lover

PAR: 30 minutes   MEDAL SCORE: 18 minutes

O'V PQYTNBQ IOPQ KTNY

—— ——————— ———— ————

HYTVOWRW DCJ IOPQ KTNY

———————— ——— ———— ————

AOWWRW, NCPOX KTN DYR

—————— ————— ——— ———

PQYTNBQ IOPQ KTNY SDCRW

——————— ———— ———— —————

DCJ VRXOWWDW.

——— ————————

Fearful Tearful

PAR: 25 minutes   MEDAL SCORE: 15 minutes

SZQ PGVVGITOS IZGOP GN

——— ————————— ————— ——

SZQ IZGOP EZX GN TUZHFFL.

——— ————— ——— —— ————————

   (DIRECTIONS FOR SOLVING CRYPTOGRAMS ARE ON PAGE 210)

ZQ GN HS EHK EGSZ ZGRNQOV;
—— —— —— ——— ———— ———————

HUP GU IXUNQCTQUIQ, ZQ GN
——— —— ——————————— —— ——

HS EHK EGSZ SZQ EXKOP.
—— ——— ———— ——— —————

Queer Bird

PAR: 49 minutes   MEDAL SCORE: 25 minutes

BD RXNTU MKQ RXNUEIZ
—— ————— ——— ———————

MXZMVZZNO. PIYN BD RXKUI
—————————— ———— —— —————

KM RXIQQD. GKC MNIQ
—— —————— ——— ————

RXIQIGUVGN.
——————————

RXIYNQVGLZD,
————————————

RXNNGVN
———————

(DIRECTIONS FOR SOLVING CRYPTOGRAMS ARE ON PAGE 210)   213

For Love of Life

PAR SCORE: 40 minutes   MEDAL SCORE: 28 minutes

LXG ZWJTXWEJMB TGCBJK WB

___ _____ _____ __

OLLCOFLGH ZR LXG NGCR

_____ __ ___ ____

TCJFGBB JI EWIG, OKH ZR

_____ __ ____ ___ __

YCJPLX JI GNGCR AOKKGC. XG

_____ __ _____ _____ __

TCGIGCB BLCMFLMCG LJ

_____ _____ __

BMAAOLWJK.

_____

     (DIRECTIONS FOR SOLVING CRYPTOGRAMS ARE ON PAGE 210)

Oh Fickle Flame

PAR SCORE: 30 minutes   MEDAL SCORE: 17 minutes

MAY THIS FEZZYDYHRY VYMBYYH

___ ____ _____ _____

U RUXDERY UHF U IEZYITHC

_ _____ ___ _ _____

XUWWETH EW MAUM MAY RUXDERY

_____ __ ____ ___ _____

IUWMW U IEMMIY ITHCYD.

_____ _ _____ _____

Anglophilia

PAR SCORE: 35 minutes   MEDAL SCORE: 18 minutes

YUIF E CEF AQ GAWIJ RO

____ _ ___ __ _____ __

SRFJRF, UI AQ GAWIJ RO SAOI;

_____ __ __ _____ __ ____

ORW GUIWI AQ AF SRFJRF ESS

___ _____ __ __ _____ ___

GUEG SAOI PEF EOORWJ.

____ ____ ___ _____

(DIRECTIONS FOR SOLVING CRYPTOGRAMS ARE ON PAGE 210)   215

Humor Us

PAR SCORE: 35 minutes   MEDAL SCORE: 20 minutes

QP WEQ SKP KER PQDI
__ ___ ___ ___ ____

KIEZMJAN EQG SKPAAN
_____ ___ _____

AEOCKIG DEQ FI EAMPCIMKIZ
_____ ___ __ _____

JZZIDAEJWEFAN FEG.
_____ ___

Divine Determination

PAR SCORE: 90 minutes   MEDAL SCORE: 60 minutes

HEKKIZ, HEZQMO, HCMEUQG,
_____ _____ _____

HINW, HLOOIH HEZIHIAQT
____ _____ _____

HITQAIZY HEQMWC HEUYIT
_____ _____ _____

(DIRECTIONS FOR SOLVING CRYPTOGRAMS ARE ON PAGE 210)

N Z L U   H Z I E H   H E M O I Z.

———— —————— ——————

H E Y P Q M O,   H L V O P W C   H V H I

———————— ———————— ————

H Q Y H E Q M Y   H L V O P;   H I U E M H Y

———————— ————— ———————

H I A L W Q L M.

————————

Evil Is Live Backwards

PAR SCORE: 35 minutes   MEDAL SCORE: 25 minutes

M E D N   Z W H   N D Q O Z L X O P   D M

———— ——— —————————— ——

K Q Z Z H,   N D O Z L O L   J L N H   E D K H E Z

—————— ———————— ———— ———————

J E L X Y   G O X H R H F,   I L E H I H R X F

————— ———————— —————————

P Z Q O Z   E X I H E,   S W D   Z D

————— —————— ——— ——

I E L N L Z X U H   W X P   K X F F X O Y

———————— ——— ————————

J W D P H   Z W H   O X J G O L N H   H R H F.

————— ——— ———————— ————

(DIRECTIONS FOR SOLVING CRYPTOGRAMS ARE ON PAGE 210)   217

Main Street, USA

Here is a simple Word Search Puzzle to cut your teeth on. If you look carefully across and down, you should be able to find all 18 cities listed below. Circle each name as you find it in the puzzle, and cross it off the list.

When you have found all of them, you will see that some letters remain unused. Write these letters, in order, in the blanks for the Secret Message, and you will find what these names have in common.

```
P  H  I  L  A  D  E  L  P  H  I  A  M  A
S  A  N  D  I  E  G  O  J  O  R  S  S  E
A  N  E  W  Y  O  R  K  G  P  O  A  R  C
T  S  W  P  O  R  T  L  A  N  D  V  M  H
O  L  O  S  A  N  G  E  L  E  S  A  I  A
N  O  R  F  O  L  K  F  V  T  H  N  A  R
B  A  L  T  I  M  O  R  E  E  U  N  M  L
O  S  E  A  T  T  L  E  S  N  I  A  I  E
S  T  A  E  D  U  L  U  T  H  D  H  S  S
T  T  N  H  O  U  S  T  O  N  A  T  E  T
O  S  S  A  N  F  R  A  N  C  I  S  C  O
N  J  A  C  K  S  O  N  V  I  L  L  E  N
```

BALTIMORE	GALVESTON	NEW ORLEANS	SAN DIEGO
BOSTON	HOUSTON	NEW YORK	SAN FRANCISCO
CHARLESTOWN	JACKSONVILLE	NORFOLK	SAVANNAH
DULUTH	LOS ANGELES	PHILADELPHIA	SEATTLE
	MIAMI	PORTLAND	

SECRET — — — — —   — — — — — — —   — —   — — —
MESSAGE: — — — — — —   — — — — — —

218

Be a Sport

If you do all things listed below, you may lose weight, and you certainly will exercise every muscle in your body. Meanwhile, exercise your brain muscle by searching vertically, horizontally, diagonally, and backwards. Circle each word as you find it.

When you have found all 28 words you will see that you have 10 letters left over that you did not use. Write these letters, in order, in the blanks and you will have the secret word.

```
B A D M I N T O N A S B
A S O C C E R C R O W I
S A R U N J A I L A I C
K I H N B O C C I E M Y
E L I H O C K E Y T E C
T S K I F O O T B A L L
B I E V C R O Q U E T E
A I E L L A B T F O S D
L A C R O S S E L X E I
L L A B Y E L L O V R R
K A R A T E T B G I W E
L W O B A S E B A L L S
```

BADMINTON	CROQUET	LACROSSE	SOCCER
BASEBALL	FOOTBALL	RACE	SOFTBALL
BASKETBALL	GOLF	RIDE	SWIM
BICYCLE	HIKE	ROW	TENNIS
BOCCIE	HOCKEY	RUN	TRACK
BOWL	JAI LAI	SAIL	VOLLEYBALL
BOX	KARATE	SKI	WRESTLE

SECRET WORD: _ _ _ _ _ _ _ _ _ _

Feathered Friends

You are no bird-brain if you can find the 25 birds hidden in this puzzle. In fact, you're probably an experienced bird watcher, used to looking up, down, sideways, across, and even backwards, which is what you have to do to find every last hidden bird. Circle them and check them off the list as you find them.

```
N  I  C  A  N  A  R  Y  L  C
I  E  O  W  L  H  E  T  O  R
B  B  R  O  A  K  N  O  O  O
O  H  L  W  R  O  T  N  N  W
R  C  K  U  C  I  E  G  P  K
G  N  T  L  E  K  O  U  I  C
O  I  A  A  C  J  E  L  G  U
O  F  G  I  K  R  A  L  E  D
S  L  H  E  R  O  N  Y  O  T
E  C  U  C  K  O  O  V  N  I
Q  U  A  I  L  T  E  R  N  S
```

BLUEJAY	EAGLE	LOON
CANARY	FALCON	ORIOLE
CHICKEN	FINCH	OWL
COOT	GOOSE	PIGEON
CROW	GULL	QUAIL
CUCKOO	HAWK	ROBIN
DOVE	HERON	TERN
DUCK	LARK	TURKEY
		WREN

Vegetable Stew

Hidden in this puzzle are the names of 27 different vegetables. To dig them out you will have to search vertically, horizontally, diagonally, and backwards. Circle and list them on a separate piece of paper as you find them. Don't get into a stew if you don't discover them all; 18 is peachy; 22 makes you a vegetarian supreme; and 25 earns you a chef's chapeau.

```
B  R  U  S  S  E  L  S  S  P  R  O  U  T  S
E  R  H  C  A  N  I  P  S  A  A  T  R  U  A
E  N  O  N  I  O  N  S  N  R  G  A  T  R  U
T  E  A  C  H  E  T  R  A  S  A  M  A  N  E
S  E  H  H  C  O  S  S  E  L  B  O  S  I  R
T  K  L  S  R  O  S  U  B  E  A  T  R  P  K
K  O  I  R  A  Q  L  M  G  Y  T  F  E  E  R
A  H  M  A  N  U  E  I  O  A  U  S  P  A  A
Y  C  A  M  N  G  Q  U  C  O  R  N  P  S  U
R  I  C  E  A  S  T  S  E  A  R  A  E  E  T
E  T  A  B  O  Y  Y  N  I  M  O  H  P  L  L
L  R  B  P  O  T  A  T  O  E  S  P  S  S  E
E  A  R  K  O  T  N  A  L  P  G  G  E  U  A
C  A  U  L  I  F  L  O  W  E  R  R  O  S  M
```

221

Answers

BODY ENGLISH . . . . page 8

1. Hands
2. Heart
3. Fingers, toes
4. Skin
5. Eyes
6. Teeth
7. Ears
8. Lip
9. Feet
10. Chin
11. Ankle
12. Neck
13. Elbow
14. Face
15. Tongue
16. Throat
17. Thumb
18. Belly
19. Limb
20. Legs
21. Arm
22. Chest
23. Calf
24. Shoulder
25. Hair
26. Chinny chin chin
27. Cheeks
28. Nose
29. Fist
30. Lung
31. Liver
32. Wrist
33. Kidney
34. Nails
35. Bones
36. Sole
37. Butt
38. Heel
39. Tooth
40. Heart, Stomach

ON ICE . . . . page 10

1. Lice or mice
2. Iceland
3. Triceratops
4. *Alice in Wonderland*
5. Nicety
6. Rice
7. Vice President
8. *Of Mice and Men*
9. Spice
10. Price
11. Iceberg
12. Trice
13. Break the ice
14. Bicentennial
15. License
16. *The Iceman Cometh*
17. Device
18. Triceps
19. Ice skating
20. Licorice

21. Slice
22. Choice
23. Precipice
24. Nice
25. Vice Squad
26. Advice
27. Entice
28. Reticent
29. Priceless
30. Leontyne Price
31. Licentious
32. *The Voice of the Turtle*

A RUN FOR YOUR MONEY . . . . page 12

1. Runaway
2. Bull Run
3. Dry run
4. In the long run
5. *Take the Money and Run*
6. Run down
7. Runcible spoon
8. Run into
9. Run-of-the-mill
10. Run the gauntlet
11. Runabout
12. Home run
13. Run a temperature
14. Run rings around
15. Run out of
16. Runway
17. Brunch
18. Damon Runyon
19. Forerunner
20. Runnymede

THE NIGHT GAME . . . . page 13

1. Fly-by-night
2. *In the Heat of the Night*
3. Nightgown
4. Night owl
5. Knights of Columbus
6. Florence Nightingale
7. *A Hard Day's Night*

222

8. One-night stand
9. *Long Day's Journey into Night*
10. *Twelfth Night*
11. *Tender Is the Night*
12. "The Night Watch"
13. Nightclub
14. "The Night Before Christmas"
15. Nightcap
16. *A Midsummer Night's Dream*
17. *The Night of the Iguana*
18. *A Little Night Music*
19. Nightshade
20. *The 1001 Arabian Nights*
21. "The Midnight Ride of Paul Revere"

WE'LL GIVE YOU A CUE . . . . page 14

1. Quack
2. Queen
3. Quirk
4. Quick
5. Quiet
6. Quest
7. Quite
8. Quasi
9. Quaff
10. Queer
11. Quail
12. Quote
13. Quota
14. Quart
15. Quill
16. Quoth
17. Query
18. Qualm
19. Quilt
20. Quell
21. Quash
22. Quake
23. Queue
24. Quire
25. Quoit
26. Quant
27. Quern

THE LITTLE THINGS . . . . page 16

1. Muffet
2. Tenderness
3. The world
4. Heaven
5. A lot
6. You cry
7. Hurts
8. Dangerous thing
9. Dog (or girl)
10. Orphan
11. Rock
12. Buttercup
13. Its own
14. Prayer
15. Girl
16. Lies
17. Children
18. Horn
21. Lead
22. Curl
23. Bethlehem
24. Oaks
25. Pitchers
26. New York
27. Lamb
28. Snips, snails
29. Cat feet
30. Girls
31. Doo
32. Near shore
33. Your horn
34. Jack Horner
35. Lamb
36. Pot
37. Know
38. Give, take, poor heart break

19. Acorns
20. Jug
39. Bo Peep
40. Slave

SOUND-ALIKE PAIRS . . . . page 18

1. Nose knows
2. Fair fare
3. Great grate
4. Two too
5. Ate eight
6. Foul fowl
7. Pale pail
8. They're there
9. Some sum
10. Aloud allowed
11. Fill Phil
12. Stayed staid
13. Rose rows
14. Ante Aunty
15. Flower flour
16. Sells cells
17. Cruise crews
18. Cash cache
19. Male mail
20. Real reel
21. Right rite
22. Hear here
23. Blew blue
24. Mean mien
25. Hoarse horse
26. Principle principal
27. New gnu
28. Prose pros

TAKE IT TO HEART. . . . . page 20

1. Heart skips a beat
2. Heartland
3. Heartache, heartbreak
4. Heartwarming
5. *Miss Lonelyhearts*
6. Hearth
7. Heart attack
8. Heart-to-heart talk
9. Heartrending
10. Learn by heart
11. "I Left My Heart in San Francisco"
12. Heart transplant
13. *Telltale Heart*
14. "You Gotta Have Heart"
15. Bighearted, kindhearted
16. Sgt. Pepper's Lonely-hearts Club Band
17. Dishearten
18. Eat one's heart out
19. *The Heart Is a Lonely Hunter*
20. Pour out one's heart
21. *Heart of the Matter*
22. Heartburn
23. *Heart of Darkness*
24. *Hearts and Minds*
25. "Sweetheart of Sigma Chi"

223

NO HOLDS BARRED. . . . . .page 21

1. Barbra Streisand
2. Barbaric
3. Barrow Gang
4. Barbecue
5. Barbershop quartet
6. Barbiturate
7. Barclays Bank
8. Bard of Avon
9. Barricuda
10. Barley
11. Bartender
12. Barbarossa
13. Embark
14. Barabbas
15. Embarrass
16. Sybarite
17. Barbary Coast
18. Clara Barton
19. Crowbar
20. Disbar
21. Embargo
22. Barnstormer
23. Barrel-roll

MOONGAZING. . . . . .page 22

1. "Moon over Miami"
2. "Moonlight" Sonata
3. "Moon River"
4. Moon Mullins
5. *Half Moon*
6. "Blue Moon"
7. Once in a blue moon
8. Tom Mooney
9. Moonshine
10. *Teahouse of the August Moon*
11. Rev. Sun Myung Moon
12. Moonlight
13. *Moon for the Misbegotten*
14. *The Moonstone*
15. *The Moon and Sixpence*
16. *From the Earth to the Moon*
17. "Moonlight Serenade"
18. Man in the moon
19. *The Moonspinners*
20. *Paper Moon*
21. "Fly Me to the Moon"

22. Mooncalf or moonraker
23. Shoot the moon
24. Baying at the moon

ABOUT FACE. . . . . .page 23

1. Deface
2. Barefaced
3. Facelift
4. Facet
5. Efface
6. Face the music or Face up to
7. Facetious
8. Preface
9. Scarface
10. Red-faced
11. Surface
12. Two-faced
13. Boldface
14. Pull a long face
15. Face-to-face
16. Face value
17. Face-off
18. Save face
19. Paleface
20. Open-faced
21. "The Face on the Barroom Floor"
22. *The Three Faces of Eve*
23. Elroy Face
24. *Face to Face*

EAT, DRINK, AND BE MERRY . . . .page 24

1. Corn
2. Milk
3. Bananas
4. Tarts
5. Blueberry
6. Tea
7. Cabbages
8. Honey, vinegar
9. Turkey
10. Fish
11. Lollipops or wine
12. Molasses
13. Pike
14. Pear
15. Apple
16. Chowder
17. Beer
18. Eggs
19. Mustard (Ice)
20. Cream
21. Sugar, Spice
22. Sugar
23. Pie
24. Stew
25. Milk, Honey
26. Bean
27. Lemon
28. Beet
29. Bass
30. Peanuts,

224

29. Teapot
30. Counter
31. Cabinet
32. Vacuum
33. *Mattress*
34. Candlestick

35. Glass
36. Radio
37. Razor
38. Screen
39. Door
40. Clock

THE NAME OF THE DAME . . . . . . page 26

1. Peg	23. Mary
2. Maggie	24. Mildred
3. Molly	25. Linda
4. Jeanine	26. Stella
5. Lucy	27. Rose
6. Kate	28. Pauline
7. Annie	29. Jeannie
8. Zuleika	30. Sue
9. Heloise	31. Eileen
10. Diana	32. Daisy
11. Cleopatra	33. Eugénie
12. Irene	34. Virginia
13. Alice	35. Bernadette
14. Louise	36. Hedda
15. Susie	37. Jane
16. Anna	38. Carrie
17. Bonnie	39. Kitty
18. Dolly	40. Eve
19. Lily	41. Lorna
20. Josephine	42. Maud
21. Irma	43. Manon
22. Eleanor	44. Juliet

AROUND THE HOUSE. . . . . page 28

1. Fork	15. Bureau
2. Broom	16. Spoon
3. Tables	17. Iron
4. Closet	18. Lamps
5. Telephone	19. Curtain
6. Range	20. Bowl
7. Kitchen sink	21. Chair
8. Davenport	22. Table
9. Pot, kettle	23. Cupboard
10. Pitchers	24. Bed
11. Mirror	25. Candle
12. Frying pan	26. Dish
13. Plate	27. Spread
14. Tub	28. Cup

PLAY YOUR CARD. . . . . page 30

1. Cardiograph	12. Calling card
2. Place card	13. Benjamin
3. Discard	Cardozo
4. Cardinal	14. St. Louis
5. Lay all one's	Cardinals
cards on the	15. Cardamom
table	16. Cardiff
6. Card catalogue	17. Cardigan
7. Bacardi	18. Card sharp
8. Cardiac arrest	19. Ricky Ricardo
9. Placard	20. Valéry Giscard
10. Cardoon	d'Estaing
11. Face card	

HORSING AROUND. . . . . page 31

1. *Horse Feathers*
2. "A horse! A horse! My kingdom for a horse!"
3. White Horse
4. A horse of different color
5. Get a horse!
6. Don't look a gift horse in the mouth
7. *They Shoot Horses, Don't They?*
8. Long horse (or, side horse)
9. Stalking-horse
10. Workhorse
11. Horsefly
12. Horse chestnut
13. Dark horse
14. The Trojan Horse
15. Horseless carriages

PUNS FOR FUN . . . . page 32

1. Hostel	6. Clique
2. Inveighed	7. Cygnet
3. Lei	8. Genes
4. Lichens	9. Fissure
5. Marshal	10. Flex

11. Balm
12. Bey
13. Knave
14. Duct
15. Yew
16. Cache
17. Offal
18. Boulder
19. Cozen
20. Phrase
21. Hied
22. Frieze

23. Plait
24. Spayed
25. Sioux
26. Bridle
27. Faze
28. Rued
29. Nix
30. Brood
31. Main
32. Lynx
33. Taught

FANFARE . . . . page 34

1. Fandango
2. Fancy-free
3. *White Fang*
4. Faneuil Hall
5. Fan mail
6. Infant
7. *Fanny Hill*
8. Trip the light fantastic
9. Fantasy
10. Fanatic
11. Fanny Brice
12. Infantry
13. Fan-tan

14. Fan the flames
15. Profane
16. *Fantasticks*
17. *Fantasia*
18. *Cosi Fan Tutte*
19. *Fantastic Voyage*
20. Fanback
21. Newfangled
22. Tiffany
23. *Enfant terrible*
24. Sulfanilamide
25. Bouffant

MOTHER LODE . . . . page 36

1. Implore
2. Stevedore
3. Galore
4. Lahore
5. Shore
6. Semaphore
7. Aforementioned
8. Oregon
9. Singapore
10. Heretofore
11. Adore
12. Oread
13. Spore
14. Orestes

15. Snore
16. Deplore
17. Mores
18. Swore
19. Explore
20. Chore
21. Arboreal
22. Toreador
23. Eyesore
24. Reforestation
25. Coreligionist
26. Foreign
27. Choreographer
28. Carnivore

RHYMING EXPRESSIONS . . . . page 38

1. Deadhead
2. Boob tube
3. Blackjack
4. Sweetmeats
5. Hurdy-gurdy
6. Claptrap
7. Willy-nilly
8. Hotshot
9. Hanky-panky
10. Helter-skelter
11. Tutti-frutti
12. Wingding
13. Hootchie-kootchie
14. Fat cat
15. Hocus-pocus
16. Mumbo-jumbo
17. Hoi polloi
18. Fuddy-duddy
19. Namby-pamby
20. Harum-scarum
21. Kowtow
22. Wear and tear
23. Pell-mell

24. Hobnob
25. Jeepers creepers
26. Honky-tonk
27. Hi-fi
28. Huff and puff
29. Voodoo
30. Hubbub
31. Hodgepodge
32. Bee's knees
33. Nearest and dearest
34. True blue
35. Fair and square
36. Pie in the sky
37. Fourscore
38. Heebie-jeebies
39. Plain Jane
40. Prime time
41. Fleet Street
42. Boo-hoo
43. Late date
44. Night flight
45. May Day

WHAT'S IN A WORD? . . . . page 40

1. Joy
2. Uncompromising
3. Meddler
4. Ignorance
5. Trite
6. Hater of mankind
7. Privilege
8. Irritable
9. Subordinate ruler
10. Legislator
11. Extreme

12. Commonplace remark
13. Of doubtful authenticity
14. Outgoing
15. Resentment
16. Aggravate
17. Wangle
18. Punish
19. Ban
20. Lavishly ornate

THE STORY OF MAN . . . . page 42

1. Manhattan
2. Manhole
3. *The Man Who Would Be King*
4. Mandrill
5. Manicure
6. Necromancy
7. Mantel

8. Manna
9. Reprimand
10. *A Man for All Seasons*
11. Mandarin
12. Mandolin
13. Thomas Mann
14. Mandatory
15. Man o' War
16. Foreman
17. Mandate
18. Commando
19. Manifesto
20. Emancipation Proclamation
21. Manganese
22. Manacles
23. Manager
24. Mantilla
25. *The Man without a Country*
26. Manual
27. Manuscript
28. Manufacturer
29. Comanches
30. Manila
31. Mantua
32. *The Woman I Love*
33. Manure
34. Mannequin
35. Manchester
36. Manipulate
37. Amanuensis
38. Semantics

OF THEE I SING . . . . page 44

1. Thermometer
2. Theta
3. Zither
4. Pathetic
5. *Gone with the Wind*
6. Theft
7. Feathers
8. Lathe
9. Theatre
10. Othello
11. Bathe
12. Theme
13. Thespian
14. Thebes
15. Theology
16. Heathen
17. Leather
18. Mother Nature
19. Matthew
20. Mathematics
21. *Blithe Spirit*
22. Athens
23. Seethe
24. Loathe
25. Theory
26. Scythe
27. Thermos

28. *The Iceman Cometh*
29. Catherine
30. Writhe

DOUBLE TROUBLE . . . . page 46

1. Tend, end
2. Swallow, wallow
3. Trail, rail
4. Goat, oat
5. Bear, ear
6. Grouse, rouse
7. Boar, oar
8. Weasel, easel
9. Orange, range
10. Agate, gate
11. Marrow, arrow
12. Breed, reed
13. Fair, air
14. Sports, ports
15. Tram, ram
16. Cart, art
17. Track, rack
18. Hold, old
19. Cowl, owl
20. Burn, urn
21. Trust, rust
22. Clean, lean
23. Prim, rim
24. Sample, ample
25. Spar, par
26. Flower, lower
27. Thorn, horn
28. Scare, care
29. Shone, hone
30. Price, rice
31. Opinion, pinion
32. Wring, ring
33. Wrote, rote
34. Craze, raze
35. Cease, ease

X MARKS THE SPOT . . . . page 49

1. Chicago White Sox
2. Halifax
3. Karl Marx
4. Coccyx
5. Sphinx
6. Paradox
7. Anthrax
8. Phoenix
9. Appomattox
10. William Bendix
11. Tyrannosaurus Rex
12. Beaux
13. Larynx
14. Lester Maddox
15. Chicken pox
16. Hex
17. *Mannix*
18. Convex
19. Bordeaux
20. Syntax

FIND THE AUTHOR . . . . page 50

1. Willie Maykit
2. Helen Hiwadder
3. Rufus Caving
4. Thomasina Tournament
5. Sue Nora Lador
6. R. Hugh Cumming
7. Judy Fiant
8. Phillipa Karef
9. Lord Howard Hertz
10. Claude Foote
11. Hedda DeClasse

MR. FARMER'S FARM . . . . page 51

Mr. Carter—ploughman

Mr. Carter's son—Mr. Ploughman's (shepherd's) apprentice

Mr. Driver—carter

Mr. Driver's son—Mr. Carter's (ploughman's) apprentice

Mr. Ploughman—shepherd

Mr. Ploughman's son—Mr. Shepherd's (driver's) apprentice

Mr. Shepherd—driver

Mr. Shepherd's son—Mr. Driver's (carter's) apprentice

From clue 1 we can assume that the carter's apprentice is neither young Ploughman (since he can't be marrying his own sister) nor young Carter (given). But the carter's apprentice cannot be young Driver, because young Driver is an only child; thus the carter's apprentice must be Mr. Shepherd's son.

Mr. Shepherd cannot be the shepherd (given) or the ploughman (since clue 3 says he's married to the ploughman's mother); nor can he be the carter, since his son is the carter's apprentice. He must therefore be the driver.

Since the carter cannot be Mr. Ploughman (clue 2) nor Mr. Carter (given), he must be Mr. Driver. The ploughman, then, must be Mr. Carter, and his apprentice must be young Driver. Mr. Ploughman must therefore be the shepherd, and his apprentice must be young Carter. Young Ploughman can only be the driver's apprentice.

THE BLIND MAN SEES . . . . page 52

The blind man reasoned thus: If there were a black hat on my head and a black hat on the head of the second speaker, then the first man addressed would have seen two black hats. He would have then drawn the inescapable conclusion that his own hat was white.

Similarly, if there were a black hat on my own head and a black hat on the head of the first man addressed, then the second speaker would have known that his own hat was white. Since neither of these men were able to draw any conclusion, it is clear that I do not wear a black hat *in combination with someone else wearing a black hat.*

The only question left then for me is:— Do I *alone* wear a black hat? If I did, the second speaker would see it and would have been able to conclude definitely the color of his own hat. The second speaker would have said to himself, "My hat is not black, for if it were, the first speaker would have seen two black hats and would have known that *his* hat was white. Therefore, my hat cannot be black."

But the second speaker was not able to draw this conclusion. He could only have failed to do this because he did not see a black hat on my head. Therefore, since I and another do not wear black hats and since I do not wear a black hat all by myself, there must be a white hat on my head.

THE COUNTERFEIT COIN . . . . page 52

Two. The wise man divided the nine coins into three groups of three. First he weighed Group A against Group B. If they balanced, then he knew that each of the coins in these groups were of the same weight, and therefore each of these six coins were made of pure gold.

The counterfeit would then be found in the last group of three. He then took any two of the last three remaining coins, and put one of these two coins on each side of the scale. If these two coins balanced, then the counterfeit coin would have to be the last unweighed coin. If the two coins did not balance, then of course, the lighter coin—the one on the scale that went up—would be the counterfeit coin.

Now suppose that in the first instance, when weighing the two groups of three, one side of the scale went up. It would then be clear that the lighter coin was among this group of three. The sage would then proceed as stated above, weighing two of the three coins among which the lightest one was to be found.

TRUTH IN LABELING .... page 53

Make a grid with the five jar numbers across the top. Along the side, write What, Who, and When. Enter in the grid the information contained in clues 4, 6, 8, 11, 13, and 1.

Number	1	2	3	4	5
What	sweet pickles	corn			
Who	Lois	Pat	Kris		Carol
When					

Now deduce from the remaining clues the information to complete the grid. Since Maggie is the only unidentified donor, she must have given jar #4, which was canned in 1973 (clue 7). Clue 14 indicates that jar #3 has green beans, and therefore jar #5 must have grape juice. Clue 9 dates jar #2. Clue 15 dates jar #5. Clue 3 dates jar #3, which leaves clue 10 to date jar #1. Thus the information in the grid should read as follows: Jar #1 was given by Lois in 1969 and contains sweet pickles. Jar #2 contains corn and was given by Pat in 1972. Jar #3 contains green beans which Kris gave Ann in 1974. Jar #4 was given in 1973 by Maggie and contains tomato juice. Jar #5 contains grape juice and was given by Carol in 1971.

TYPING TROUBLE .... page 54

Reading through the clues we see that the letters on the keys are: BC, DF, JK, GH, NP,

and LM. Make a grid with these letter combinations across the top. On the side write Number and Symbol. Now enter into the grid the information given in clues 1, 2, 4, 6, and 10.

Letter	BC	DF	JK	GH	NP	LM
Number	77				26	
Symbol		@	&			•

Now you have to deduce from the remaining clues the numbers and symbols that go with the letters. Clue #3 tells that LM cannot be 5; and from clue #7 we know that it is not 92 either. LM must therefore be either 36 or 94; but clue #8 says it is not 36, so it must be 94. Since GH is the only key to which we have not yet assigned a number or a symbol, it is the only key that will fit clue #8; thus, GH must go with 36 and $. Clue #9 tells that since 26 ≠ #, 77 must be #. And clue #11 establishes, by the same reasoning, that @ must be 92. Which leaves 5 for JK, and % for NP. To recapitulate, BC and 77 and # go together; DF and 92 and @ go together; JK and 5 and & go together; GH goes with 36 and $; NP goes with 26 and %; and LM goes with 94 and •.

THE RIGHT TYPE .... page 55

Reading through the clues we see that the capital letter combinations are: PT, LM, DF, ZQ, and XY. Make a grid with these letters across the top, and Lower case letters, Numbers, and Symbols along the side. Fill in the information contained in clues 1, 3, 5, 10, and 12.

Cap letters	PT	LM	DF	ZQ	XY
Lower case letters	ou		ao		
Numbers					23
Symbols			#		•

Now go back over the remaining clues and by deduction fill in the missing information. Clue 6 tells that XY goes with $, and it there-

fore also goes with ie (clue 11). This leaves ¢
for either PT or DF, but clue 14 tells that
¢ ≠DF, so ¢ must = PT, leaving % for DF.
Clue 9 now tells us that DF = 16, and clue 4
tells that 70 = PT. Clue 13 tells that LM ≠35,
so ZQ must = 35; which leaves 68 and ae
(clue 8) for LM. To recapitulate, the keyboard reads as follows: PT goes with ou, 70,
¢; LM goes with ae, 68, #; DF goes with ao,
16, %; ZQ goes with eu, 35, *; XY goes with
ie, 23, $.

MELTING POT . . . . page 56

Reading through the clues, you find the
names of the five men are: Pete, Ed, Paul,
Chris, and Andy. Make a grid with these
names on top, and Country and Occupation
on the side. The information given in
clues 1, 7, 8, and 9 can be filled in the grid.

	P	E	Pl	C	A
Country	Greece		England		
Occupa-tion				eng.	teacher

By deduction, you can now complete the
grid. Clue #5 establishes Paul as a tailor.
Since Pete is from Greece, clue #3 marks Ed
as a carpenter from Italy. Thus, Pete must be
the doctor. If Chris is not from Iceland (clue
#6), Andy must be. Thus, Chris must be
from Norway. You have now completed the
grid: Pete is a doctor from Greece; Ed a carpenter from Italy; Paul a tailor from England; Chris an engineer from Norway; and
Andy a teacher from Iceland.

CAMPUS FUN . . . . page 56

Reading through the clues, you find that the
names of the colleges are: State University,
Compass College, United American University, Central State College. Make a grid and
write these names across the top. Write
Team, Colors, and Sport along the side. Now
fill the information given in clues 1, 2, 4, 6
and 7 in the grid.

	State U	Compass	United American	Central State
Team		Bulls	Bears	
Colors	blue & white		yellow & blue	
Sport				track

Now, by deduction you should be able to use
the remaining clues to complete the grid.
Clue #3 tells that the sport at United
American is baseball. Clue #5 establishes
State U's team as Bobcats, and their sport as
football, since the only other college whose
team name we don't know is Central State,
but its sport is track. We can now use clue #8
to deduce that Central's team must be the
Canaries, and its colors are yellow and
brown; which leaves clue #9 to tell that
Compass excels in swimming and wears tan
and green. To recapitulate, the completed
grid now shows: State U's team is the
Bobcats, who play football and wear blue
and white; Compass' team is the Bulls, who
wear tan and green, and swim; United
American has the Bears, who wear yellow
and blue, and play baseball; and Central
State has the Canaries, who wear yellow and
brown, and excel at track.

MATCH THEM UP . . . . page 57

The six Senators are: Clawson, Jones, Henry,
Johnson, Rooney, and Smith. Make a grid
and write these names on top, with Wife,
State, and Bill along the side. Fill in the information contained in clues 2, 4, 6, 8, 9, 11,
and 13.

Senator	C	J	H	J	R	S
Wife	Jill				Corrine	
State	Idaho	Ohio	Georgia			
Bill	Mil. Ath.		Empl. Handi.			Fed. Library

Now, deduce from the other clues the information to complete the chart. Since the only
three remaining states are Indiana, Maine

and Utah, clue 7 tells that Johnson must be from Maine. Therefore, clue 1 indicates that Senator Smith is married to Peggy and is from Utah, which means Senator Rooney must be from Indiana and his bill is about St. Patrick's Day (clue 10). Clue 5 now shows that Senator Johnson's proposed bill is on the National Leaf. Clue 12 means that Senator Jones' bill is about bussing, since this is the only bill left unassigned, and his wife is Mary. Clue 14 makes Kathy Senator Johnson's wife, leaving Jane for Senator Henry. To recapitulate, Senator Clawson is from Idaho and his wife is Jill, and his bill is on military athletics. Senator Jones who is married to Mary, comes from Ohio and is proposing a bill on school busing. Senator Henry is married to Jane; they live in Georgia; and his proposal is about employing the handicapped. Senator Johnson's bill is on the National Leaf; his wife is Kathy, and they live in Maine. Senator Rooney is married to Corrine; they live in Indiana, and the Senator's bill is about St. Patrick's Day. Senator Smith, who is from Utah, is sponsoring a bill about a federal library, and is married to Peggy.

THE FIVE OFFICE BOYS . . . . page 58

	Read-ing	Writ-ing	Arith-metic	Geog-raphy	His-tory	Total
Les	2	3	4	3	0	12
Oscar	1	2	3	4	1	11
George	4	1	1	2	2	10
Ira	0	4	2	0	3	9
Chuck	3	0	0	1	4	8

Since each of the boys received a 4 in one subject, Les' can only be in arithmetic. Scores of 1 and 0 are left to be given to Oscar and Ira in reading; the 0 cannot be Oscar's because of clue E, so he must receive the 1 and Ira the 0.

George's scores in writing and arithmetic are the same and are not 0's (B). Since scores of 2, 3 and 4 points are already

entered in those columns, his scores in writing and arithmetic must be 1's. Under writing and arithmetic, Chuck and Oscar are the only boys with no scores yet. They must split a 0 and a 2 in writing and a 0 and a 3 in arithmetic. We know from E, though, that Oscar got no 0's, so Chuck must get both of them; Oscar thus gets a 2 in writing and a 3 in arithmetic. Chuck's 4 in history must equal his other scores combined (clue F), so therefore his geography score must be 1.

George's scores in geography and history must be equal but may not be 0. Scores of 1, 3 and 4 are already used in those columns, so his scores in these subjects must be 2. Ira's geography score must then be 0.

Chuck, who came in last, has 8 points. Ira's score must then be at least 9, and his history score has to be 3.

Oscar outscored Les in two subjects (clue E). One of them, geography, is already evident; the other must be history. The only scores left are 1 and 0, so the 0 must be Les'.

MILITARY SECRETS . . . . page 59

	Bob	Sam	Tom	Ken
State	Utah	Kansas	Maine	Ohio
Hobby	Dancing	Stamps	Baseball	Cards
Service	Army	Air Force	Marines	Navy

From clues 1, 3, 4 and 9, the grid can immediately be filled in with Bob's home state (Utah), Sam's home state (Kansas), Tom's hobby (baseball) and Ken's service (Navy). We know from clue 2 that dancing and the Army will go in the same column; Tom's hobby and Ken's service are established, so Bob and Sam are the possibilities for Army and dancing. We know, however, from #5 that the Army cannot be in the same column with Kansas, so Bob must be the Army man who likes to dance. Clue 10 says the Marine is from Maine, and Tom is the only serviceman still without service or home state, so he has to be the Marine from Maine. Sam is now the only one without a service branch, thus he has to be the flyer; Ken is now the only one left without a home state, so he has to be from Ohio. Clue #8 can now only mean that Ken is the card player, and we are left with Sam as the stamp collector of clue #6.

THE BLIND ABBOT . . . . page 60

18 monks

1	0	8
0		0
8	0	1

20 monks

4	1	4
1		1
4	1	4

24 monks

3	3	3
3		3
3	3	3

32 monks

1	7	1
7		7
1	7	1

36 monks

0	9	0
9		9
0	9	0

PAPA'S PLANTS . . . . page 60

Reading through the clues you see that the four plants are: African violet, spider, philodendron, and coleus. Make a chart with these names across the top. Along the side, write Room, Pot Color, and Direction. The information from the following clues can be entered in the appropriate boxes of the chart: #1, #5, #10, #11, #9, #7.

	African Violet	Spider	Philo-dendron	Coleus
Room			Den	Kitchen
Pot Color				Green
Direction	North	East		South

You will note that only one direction is missing; therefore the philodendron must have a west window. Now go through the clues again, and by deduction, complete the boxes of the chart. Clue #8 implies that the African violet must be in the living room; and therefore the spider plant must be in the playroom. Clue #3 thus tells that the spider plant is in a red pot. Clues #2 & 4 show that the African violet is in a yellow pot, and the philodendron is in a blue pot.

THE ADVENTUROUS SNAIL . . . . . . page 61

Twenty days.

At the end of 17 days the snail will have climbed 17 feet, and at the end of the 18th day it will be at the top of the wall. It instantly begins slipping while sleeping, and will be two feet down the other side at the end of the 18th night. How long will it take to travel the remaining 18 feet? If it slips two feet at night it clearly overcomes the tendency to slip two feet during the daytime, in climbing up. (In rowing up a river we have the stream against us, but in coming down it is with us and helps us.) If the snail can climb three feet and overcome the tendency to slip two feet in 12 hours' ascent, it could with the same exertion crawl five feet a day on the level. Therefore, in going down, the same exertion carries the snail seven feet in 12 hours; that is, five feet by personal exertion and two feet by slip. This, with the night slip, gives it a descending progress of nine feet in 24 hours. It can therefore do the remaining 18 feet in exactly two days, and the whole journey up and down will take the snail exactly 20 days.

TYPESETTER'S HEADACHE . . . . . . page 62

Reading through the clues you see that the letter combinations are: XY, TR, LK, and ES. Make a chart with these letters across the top, and Symbol and Number along the side. Clues #1, 2, and 3 can be entered into the appropriate boxes on the chart.

232

	XY	TR	LK	ES
Number	57			
Symbol		$	%	

By deduction you can use the remaining clues to complete the chart. Since TR and LK already have symbols, and XY already has a number, clue #5 must relate to ES. This leaves the symbol # for XY. If LK is not 39 (clue #7), TR must be 39 and LK must be 68.

TYPESETTER'S NIGHTMARE...... page 63

Reading through the clues you see that the consonant combinations are: ST, FG, LK, ZX, and MN. Make a chart with these letters at the top, and with the Number, Symbol and Vowel along the side. The information from clues #1, 4, 5, 9, 11, 6, and 3 can be put in the appropriate boxes of the chart.

	ST	FG	LK	ZX	MN
Number	56		13	79	
Symbol			!		
Vowel		i	u		o

By deduction, the information in the rest of the clues can be used to complete the chart. If (clue #2) 28 does not go with FG, it must belong with MN, and therefore FG must go with the only remaining number 98. If (clue #13) a doesn't go with ZX, it must go with ST; and thus ST must go with % (clue #10). This leaves e for ZX. So ZX must go with # (clue #7). Now clues #8 and 12 establish that MN goes with *, and FG goes with &.

THE LONESOME PRAIRIE .... page 64

Clues 1, 3, 5, 6, 7, 9, 12, and 14 go in right away; clue 15 follows immediately since we know who the Oklahoman is (clue 12).

	Horse	Hat	Home
Barney	Blue	blue	Wyoming
Cal	Red River	green	Utah
Chuck	Patches	red	Texas
Del	Blaze	brown	Colorado
Slim	Berry	tan	Oklahoma
Al	Ringo	yellow	Nevada

Al is the only cowboy with neither a horse nor a state, so he must be the Nevadan who rides Ringo (clue 10). Del has neither hat nor state, so clue 11 must be about him. By elimination Chuck has to be the Texan.

From clue 4 we can be sure that the green hat is Cal's and his horse is Red River (clue 13). Clue 2 then makes it clear that Barney's hat is blue and his horse is Blue.

THE SOCCER TOURNAMENT ...... page 65

Teams	Score
Central-Madison...........	3-4
Central-Lakeside	4-1
Central-Western...........	0-0
Madison-Lakeside..........	1-0
Madison-Western	0-0
Lakeside-Western	0-0

If Western scored no goals at all but still ended the tournament with three points, it must have held all three of its opponents to 0-0 ties.

Of Central's total of seven goals, four were scored against Lakeside and none against Western, so it must have scored three points against Madison.

Since Madison has a total of five points and one of them is the tie with Western, it had to win its games with Central and Lakeside. One must keep in mind, however, that all the goals scored in the Central-Madison, Central-Lakeside and Madison-Lakeside games have to total thirteen. The Central-Lakeside game accounts for five, and Central's goals in the Central-Madison game bring the total already to eight. Madison's score in the Central-Madison game must then be four, and Madison can only have beaten Lakeside 1-0.

VARIETY IS THE SPICE . . . . page 66

	Doro.	Geo.	Earl	Walt
Cuisine	Mex.	Ital.	Fr.	Chin.
Subject	math	Eng.	geo.	Fr.
State	Ind.	Ind.	Ore.	Tex.

Clues 4 and 10 can be entered immediately, and clue 10 also provides a spot for clue 7. George must be from Indiana, and Dorothy must also (clue 1). Clue 2's French teacher from Texas must be Walt, since he alone is left without a state or a subject.

Clue 5's math teacher must then be Dorothy. Clue 9's French food fan from Oregon must be Earl. Since clue 3 says the English teacher, who is George, is not the Chinese food fan, it must be Walt. Therefore George must prefer Italian food.

SUGAR AND SPICE . . . . page 67

	Bag	Boy-friend	TV Show
Lois	red	Scott	M*A*S*H
Mary	blue	Ben	Happy Days
Margie	yel.	Andy	Hawaii 5-0
Shirley	grn.	Ed	Lav. & Shirley
Diane	blk.	Al	Maude
Sharon	pld.	Ken	American Bandstand

Clues 1, 3, 4, 5, 7, 11, and 12 provide immediate entries for the matrix. It is evident at once from clues 2 and 11 that Sharon is Ken's girlfriend. Shirley's column is the only one with neither a sleeping bag nor a boyfriend, so she must be Ed's girlfriend and have a green bag (clue 6).

Lois and Margie do not yet have sleeping bags assigned; from clue 9, then, we know that Lois' is red, and from clue 11, that the yellow must be Margie's.

Mary has neither boyfriend nor TV show beneath her name, so clue 10 must pertain to her. Maude and Hawaii 5-0 are the only programs left and must be assigned to Margie and Diane; clue 8 makes clear which show goes to which girl.

234

ANAMAZE . . . . page 72

The name of the game is confusing!

SPAGHETTI . . . . page 74

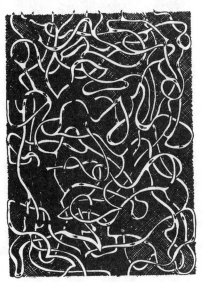

SQUARE OR CIRCLE . . . . page 76

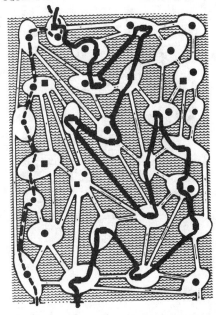

PICK UP STICKS . . . . page 78

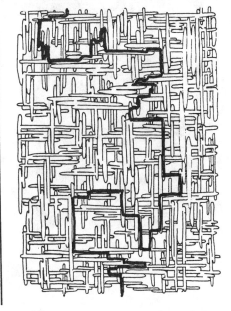

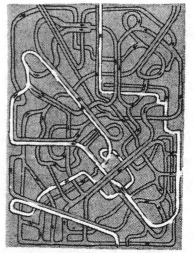

22. Pilot	36. Slop	50. Spout
23. Pint	37. Slot	51. Stop
24. Pious	38. Snip	52. Stun
25. Plot	39. Snit	53. Suction
26. Politics	40. Snot	54. Sunup
27. Post	41. Soil	55. Toil
28. Pout	42. Solicit	56. Tonic
29. Punt	43. Soul	57. Topic
30. Scion	44. Soup	58. Tulip
31. Scout	45. Spin	59. Tunic
32. Scup	46. Spit	60. Until
33. Silt	47. Split	61. Unto
34. Slip	48. Spoil	62. Unit
35. Slit	49. Spot	63. Upon

SOLDIERS . . . . page 104

1. Dire	13. Less	25. Side
2. Does	14. Lieder	26. Silo
3. Dole	15. Lode	27. Sire
4. Dose	16. Lore	28. Sled
5. Dossier	17. Lose	29. Slide
6. Dossil	18. Older	30. Soil
7. Dress	19. Ride	31. Sold
8. Dries	20. Rile	32. Solder
9. Dross	21. Rise	33. Sole
10. Idle	22. Roil	34. Solid
11. Idol	23. Role	35. Sore
12. Isle	24. Rose	

VESTIBULE . . . . page 104

1. Beet	16. Etui	31. Steel
2. Belie	17. Evil	32. Stele
3. Belt	18. Isle	33. Stile
4. Beset	19. Islet	34. Stub
5. Best	20. Lest	35. Suet
6. Bile	21. List	36. Suit
7. Bite	22. Live	37. Suite
8. Blest	23. Lube	38. Svelte
9. Blue	24. Lust	39. Tile
10. Built	25. Lute	40. Tube
11. Bust	26. Sieve	41. Utile
12. Bustle	27. Silt	42. Vest
13. Elite	28. Sleet	43. Vibes
14. Elusive	29. Slit	44. Vile
15. Elves	30. Slut	45. Vise

SHEEPISHLY . . . . page 105

1. Eely	9. Less	17. Ship
2. Espy	10. Lies	18. Sleep
3. Heel	11. Lisp	19. Slip
4. Heil	12. Peel	20. Spiel
5. Help	13. Pile	21. Spies
6. Hipless	14. Plies	22. Sylph
7. Hiss	15. Seep	23. Yelp
8. Isle	16. Sheep	24. Yipe

MEMORABILIA . . . . page 106

1. Able	35. Limber
2. Alibi	36. Limbo
3. Amber	37. Lime
4. Amble	38. Loam
5. Amoeba	39. Lobe
6. Amoral	40. Lore
7. Aroma	41. Mail
8. Bail	42. Male
9. Bale	43. Mamba
10. Balm	44. Mare
11. Bare	45. Memoir
12. Beam	46. Memorial
13. Bear	47. Mile
14. Bier	48. Mime
15. Bile	49. Mire
16. Blame	50. Miro
17. Blare	51. Mobile
18. Boar	52. Moil
19. Boil	53. Mole
20. Boiler	54. Molar
21. Bore	55. Moral
22. Brim	56. More
23. Broil	57. Oiler
24. Earl	58. Oral
25. Embalm	59. Rail
26. Embroil	60. Ramble
27. Emir	61. Real
28. Labia	62. Ream
29. Labor	63. Rial
30. Lair	64. Rile
31. Lamb	65. Rime
32. Lame	66. Roam
33. Liar	67. Robe
34. Limb	68. Role

SYCOPHANT . . . . page 107

1. Atop	22. Nosh	42. Scanty
2. Canopy	23. Nosy	43. Shanty
3. Cant	24. Notch	44. Shat
4. Cash	25. Oast	45. Shay
5. Cast	26. Oaty	46. Shop
6. Chant	27. Pact	47. Shot
7. Chanty	28. Pant	48. Snap
8. Chap	29. Past	49. Snatch
9. Chat	30. Pasty	50. Snot
10. Chop	31. Patch	51. Soap
11. Coast	32. Patsy	52. Span
12. Coat	33. Phony	53. Spat
13. Cony	34. Poach	54. Spay
14. Copy	35. Pony	55. Spot
15. Cost	36. Posh	56. Stanch
16. Cosy	37. Post	57. Stay
17. Cyst	38. Posy	58. Stony
18. Hasp	39. Python	59. Stop
19. Hasty	40. Scan	60. Tach
20. Host	41. Scant	61. Taco
21. Nasty		62. Than

SPECTACLE . . . . page 108

1. Accept	24. Leap	47. Pleat
2. Apse	25. Lease	48. Sale
3. Aspect	26. Least	49. Salt
4. Cape	27. Lest	50. Scale
5. Case	28. Pace	51. Scalp
6. Cast	29. Pact	52. Scat
7. Caste	30. Pale	53. Seal
8. Castle	31. Past	54. Seat
9. Cease	32. Paste	55. Sect
10. Clap	33. Pastel	56. Select
11. Clasp	34. Pate	57. Slap
12. Cleat	35. Peace	58. Slat
13. Ease	36. Peal	59. Slate
14. Easel	37. Peat	60. Sleep
15. East	38. Peel	61. Sleet
16. Eclat	39. Pelt	62. Space
17. Elapse	40. Pest	63. Spat
18. Elate	41. Pestle	64. Spate
19. Elect	42. Petal	65. Stale
20. Lace	43. Place	66. Staple
21. Lapse	44. Plate	67. Steal
22. Last	45. Plea	68. Steel
23. Late	46. Please	69. Steep

70. Step	72. Tale	74. Teal
71. Talc	73. Tape	75. Tease

SPOKESMAN . . . . page 109

1. Amen	18. Name	34. Pone
2. Apse	19. Nape	35. Pose
3. Aspen	20. Ness	36. Posse
4. Epsom	21. Nope	37. Sake
5. Knap	22. Nose	38. Same
6. Make	23. Oaken	39. Sane
7. Mane	24. Omen	40. Sank
8. Manse	25. Open	41. Smoke
9. Mask	26. Paeon	42. Snake
10. Mass	27. Pane	43. Snap
11. Masse	28. Pass	44. Soak
12. Mean	29. Passé	45. Soap
13. Mess	30. Peak	46. Soma
14. Moan	31. Peon	47. Some
15. Monk	32. Poem	48. Span
16. Mope	33. Poke	49. Speak
17. Moss		50. Spoke

NOTHINGNESS . . . . page 110

1. Eight	21. Intone	42. Sing (or song)
2. Ensign	22. Nest	43. Singe
3. Ethos	23. Night	44. Site
4. Gent	24. Nine	45. Snot
5. Ghost	25. Ninth	46. Sonnet
6. Gist	26. Noise	47. Stein
7. Gniess	27. None	48. Sting
8. Gone	28. Nose	49. Stone
9. Gosh	29. Nosh	50. Tennis
10. Hinge	30. Note	51. Then
11. Hint	31. Nothing	52. Thin
12. Hiss	32. Onset	53. Thine
13. Hoist	33. Sent	54. Thing
14. Hone	34. Shin	55. This
15. Honest	35. Shine	56. Thong
16. Hose	36. Shoe	57. Those
17. Host	37. Shot	58. Tine
18. Ingot	38. Sight	59. Tinge
19. Inset	39. Sign	60. Tone
20. Into	40. Signet	
	41. Sine	

239

23. Pare	45. Sard
24. Parse	46. Sear
25. Pear	47. Seed
26. Peer	48. Seep
27. Peso	49. Seer
28. Pore	50. Sera
29. Pose	51. Serape
30. Prod	52. Sere
31. Prose	53. Soap
32. Rape	54. Soar
33. Rasp	55. Soda
34. Read	56. Sore
35. Reap	57. Spade
36. Redo	58. Spar
37. Reed	59. Spare
38. Respose	60. Spear
39. Resod	61. Sped
40. Road	62. Speed
41. Rode	63. Spore
42. Rope	64. Spread
43. Rose	65. Spree
44. Sapor-	

(partial left-edge entries)
r
ed
ep
eer
Dope
Dose
Drape
. Dread
3. Drop
17. Ease
18. Epode
19. Erase
20. Erode
21. Odea
22. Opera

1. Amen	21. Meat	41. Tame
2. Arrive	22. Merit	42. Tare
3. Arum	23. Mire	43. Tart
4. Atrium	24. Mite	44. Tear
5. Attire	25. Miter	45. Term
6. Aver	26. Mitt	46. Tier
7. Avert	27. Muire	47. Time
8. Emir	28. Mutate	48. Tire
9. Emit	29. Mute	49. Tite
10. Erratum	30. Mutt	50. Tram
11. Etui	31. Mutter	51. Treat
12. Imitate	32. Rare	52. Trim
13. Irate	33. Rate	53. Trite
14. Irritate	34. Rave	54. Trivet
15. Item	35. Remit	55. True
16. Mare	36. Rime	56. Utter
17. Mart	37. Rite	57. Varier
18. Mate	38. Rive	58. Vert
19. Matter	39. River	59. Virtue
20. Mauve	40. Rivet	60. Vitiate

1. Again	21. Grain	41. Miner
2. Agar	22. Gram	42. Mirage
3. Airman	23. Grim	43. Mire
4. Amen	24. Grime	44. Name
5. Anger	25. Grin	45. Near
6. Angrier	26. Image	46. Raga
7. Area	27. Main	47. Rage
8. Aria	28. Manage	48. Rain
9. Arrange	29. Manager	49. Rang
10. Earn	30. Mane	50. Range
11. Earring	31. Mange	51. Ranger
12. Emir	32. Manger	52. Rare
13. Engram	33. Mania	53. Ream
14. Enigma	34. Mare	54. Rear
15. Gain	35. Margin	55. Reign
16. Game	36. Marine	56. Rein
17. Gamin	37. Marriage	57. Rime
18. Garner	38. Mean	58. Ring
19. Gear	39. Mien	59. Ringer
20. Germ	40. Mine	

1. Agile	20. Lair	39. Rile
2. Aisle	21. Laser	40. Rise
3. Also	22. Liar	41. Roil
4. Aril	23. Lira	42. Role
5. Arise	24. Loge	43. Rose
6. Earl	25. Lore	44. Sage
7. Else	26. Lose	45. Sail
8. Ergo	27. Ogle	46. Sale
9. Gale	28. Ogre	47. Sari
10. Gaol	29. Oiler	48. Seal
11. Gear	30. Oral	49. Sear
12. Girl	31. Orgies	50. Segar
13. Glare	32. Osier	51. Sire
14. Glories	33. Rage	52. Slag
15. Goal	34. Rail	53. Slog
16. Gore	35. Raise	54. Soar
17. Grail	36. Rale	55. Soil
18. Isle	37. Real	56. Sole
19. Lager	38. Regal	57. Sore

1. Again	3. Airman	5. Anger
2. Agar	4. Amen	6. Angrier

240

7. Gaily	23. Lain	39. Sign
8. Gall	24. Lair	40. Signal
9. Gain	25. Lily	41. Sill
10. Gill	26. Ling	42. Silly
11. Girl	27. Lingual	43. Sing
12. Clair	28. Liny	44. Slag
13. Glans	29. Lung	45. Slang
14. Gnarl	30. Nary	46. Slay
15. Grail	31. Rail	47. Sling
16. Grain	32. Rain	48. Slug
17. Gray	33. Rally	49. Snag
18. Grill	34. Ring	50. Snarl
19. Grin	35. Ruin	51. Snug
20. Guan	36. Rung	52. Sugar
21. Gull	37. Sally	53. Surly
22. Gully	38. Sang	54. Sully
		55. Yarn

85. Snide	87. Sodder	89. Sold
86. Soda	88. Soil	90. Sole
		91. Solid

GENEALOGY . . . . page 117

1. Aeon	9. Gene	17. Leggy
2. Angle	10. Glean	18. Loan
3. Eagle	11. Glee	19. Loge
4. Eggy	12. Glen	20. Lone
5. Gale	13. Goal	21. Long
6. Gang	14. Gong	22. Noel
7. Gange	15. Lane	23. Ogle
8. Gaol	16. Lean	24. Only
		25. Yegg

DANDELIONS . . . . page 116

1. Addle	29. Idle	57. Nide
2. Adenoids	30. Inland	58. Nine
3. Aide	31. Island	59. Node
4. Aisle	32. Isle	60. Noel
5. Alien	33. Laddie	61. Noise
6. Alone	34. Lade	62. None
7. Also	35. Laden	63. Nose
8. Anile	36. Ladies	64. Odea
9. Anode	37. Land	65. Olden
10. Anon	38. Lane	66. Olid
11. Aside	39. Lead	67. Sadden
12. Dais	40. Lean	68. Saddle
13. Dale	41. Lend	69. Sail
14. Dead	42. Lens	70. Sale
15. Deal	43. Lien	71. Saline
16. Dean	44. Linden	72. Sand
17. Deli	45. Line	73. Sane
18. Dial	46. Lion	74. Seal
19. Dildo	47. Load	75. Send
20. Dine	48. Loan	76. Side
21. Diode	49. Lode	77. Sidle
22. Dole	50. Loin	78. Silo
23. Dose	51. Lone	79. Sine
24. Elan	52. Lose	80. Slain
25. Eland	53. Naid	81. Sled
26. Eosin	54. Nail	82. Slid
27. Idea	55. Neon	83. Slide
28. Ideal	56. Nidal	84. Snail

MATRIMONIAL . . . . page 118

1. Alar	29. Loam	57. Normal
2. Alarm	30. Loan	58. Omit
3. Alit	31. Loin	59. Oral
4. Alma	32. Lorn	60. Rail
5. Altar	33. Mail	61. Rain
6. Alto	34. Maim	62. Rant
7. Ammo	35. Main	63. Ratio
8. Ammonia	36. Malt	64. Ration
9. Amoral	37. Mania	65. Rational
10. Anal	38. Manor	66. Rial
11. Animal	39. Mantra	67. Rialto
12. Aorta	40. Marital	68. Riata
13. Aria	41. Martial	69. Riot
14. Aroma	42. Mart	70. Roam
15. Atom	43. Matron	71. Roan
16. Atonal	44. Minor	72. Roil
17. Imam	45. Mint	73. Tail
18. Immoral	46. Moan	74. Talon
19. Immortal	47. Moat	75. Tarn
20. Iron	48. Moil	76. Tiara
21. Lair	49. Molar	77. Tiro
22. Lama	50. Moral	78. Toil
23. Lariat	51. Morn	79. Tonal
24. Liar	52. Mort	80. Torn
25. Lima	53. Mortal	81. Trail
26. Limn	54. Nail	82. Train
27. Lint	55. Natal	83. Tram
28. Lion	56. Norm	84. Trial
		85. Trim

1. Arty	14. Start	27. Tort
2. Auto	15. Stay	28. Tory
3. Ratty	16. Stoa	29. Tour
4. Roast	17. Stoat	30. Tray
5. Roust	18. Story	31. Trot
6. Rout	19. Stout	32. Trout
7. Rust	20. Stray	33. Troy
8. Rusty	21. Strut	34. Trust
9. Rutty	22. Tart	35. Trusty
10. Soar	23. Tasty	36. Tryst
11. Sort	24. Taut	37. Tsar
12. Sour	25. Toast	38. Tutor
13. Star	26. Toasty	39. Tyro

1. Barfly	8. Parfait
2. Carfare	9. Scarf
3. Dwarf	10. Starfish
4. Earful	11. Tearful
5. Farfetched	12. Warfare
6. Farflung	13. Wharf
7. Fearful	

1. Artichoke	16. Looked
2. Bespoke	17. Poke
3. Booked	18. Poker
4. Broke	19. Pokeweed
5. Broker	20. Pokey
6. Brooked	21. Provoke
7. Choke	22. Revoke
8. Choker	23. Rooked
9. Coke	24. Spoke
10. Crooked	25. Spooked
11. Evoke	26. Stoke
12. Hooked	27. Token
13. Hooker	28. Woke
14. Invoke	29. Yoke
15. Joke	30. Yokel

1. Abbot	3. Botch
2. Botany	4. Both

5. Bother	10. Robot
6. Bottle	11. Sabot
7. Bottom	12. Sabotage
8. Botulism	13. Turbot
9. Lobotomy	14. Verboten

1. Amethyst	19. Metropolis
2. Barometer	20. Mettle
3. Comet	21. Odometer
4. Diameter	22. Optometry
5. Emetic	23. Palmetto
6. Gamete	24. Parameter
7. Geometry	25. Perimeter
8. Grommet	26. Photometer
9. Helmet	27. Plummet
10. Metal	28. Something
11. Metaphysical	29. Sometimes
12. Mete	30. Speedometer
13. Meteor	31. Symmetry
14. Meter	32. Tachometer
15. Method	33. Telemetry
16. Metope	34. Thermometer
17. Metric	35. Timetable
18. Metronome	36. Trigonometry

1. Abolish	21. Holiness
2. Alcoholic	22. Hyperbolic
3. Bobolink	23. Idolize
4. Colic	24. Metropolis
5. Coliseum	25. Monolithic
6. Colitis	26. Neolithic
7. Consolidate	27. Oligarchy
8. Consoling	28. Olive
9. Cooling	29. Parabolic
10. Cosmopolitan	30. Police
11. Crinoline	31. Policy
12. Demolish	32. Polio
13. Drooling	33. Polish
14. Foliage	34. Polite
15. Folio	35. Politic
16. Fooling	36. Politics
17. Foolish	37. Polity
18. Frivolity	38. Pooling
19. Frolic	39. Schooling
20. Holiday	40. Semolina

242

41. Solid
42. Soliloquy
43. Solitary
44. Solitude
45. Spoliation
46. Stolid

47. Systolic
48. Tooling
49. Violin
50. Volition
51. Woolier

1. Afterglow
2. Clergy
3. Converge
4. Detergent
5. Diverge
6. Emerge
7. Emergency
8. Energy
9. Erg
10. Ergo

11. Evergreen
12. Fiberglass
13. Iceberg
14. Merge
15. Overgrown
16. Pergola
17. Serge
18. Sergeant
19. Undergo
20. Verge

1. Acceptable
2. Adaptable
3. Adoptable
4. Heptad
5. Heptagon
6. Heptarchy

7. Ptarmigan
8. Receptacle
9. Septa
10. Septangle
11. Septate
12. Uptake

1. Assume
2. Assumption
3. Consume
4. Consummate
5. Consummation
6. Consumption
7. Opossum
8. Presume
9. Presumption
10. Resume
11. Resumption

12. Sumac
13. Summarize
14. Summary
15. Summation
16. Summer
17. Summit
18. Summon
19. Sump
20. Sumptuary
21. Sumptuous

1. Angel
2. Anger
3. Archangel
4. Arrange

5. Avenge
6. Banged
7. Bringer
8. Change

9. Changeling
10. Congeal
11. Congenial
12. Congenital
13. Conger
14. Congestion
15. Contingent
16. Cotangent
17. Cringe
18. Danger
19. Deranged
20. Dungeon
21. Engender
22. Evangelism
23. Exchange
24. Expunge
25. Finger
26. Flange
27. Fringe
28. Ginger
29. Grange
30. Hanger
31. Harbinger
32. Hinge
33. Hunger
34. Ingest
35. Interchange
36. Linger
37. Longer

38. Lounge
39. Lozenge
40. Lunge
41. Malingerer
42. Mange
43. Manger
44. Meninges
45. Orange
46. Plangent
47. Plunge
48. Pongee
49. Pungent
50. Range
51. Ranger
52. Rearrange
53. Revenge
54. Ringer
55. Singe
56. Singer
57. Syringe
58. Tangent
59. Tinge
60. Ungentlemanly
61. Vengeance
62. Vengeful
63. Warmonger
64. Winged
65. Zinger

1. Ardent
2. Ardor
3. Arduous
4. Award
5. Backward
6. Bard
7. Bastard
8. Beard
9. Board
10. Bustard
11. Card
12. Cardamom
13. Cardinal
14. Cardoon
15. Coward

16. Custard
17. Dastardly
18. Discard
19. Disregard
20. Downward
21. Eardrum
22. Eastward
23. Fardel
24. Forward
25. Garden
26. Gardenia
27. Greensward
28. Guard
29. Hard
30. Harden

CROSSWORD PUZZLE NO. 1 . . . . . . page 128

```
O R B S   S T A I N   A C H E
M O A T   A O R T A   C O O L
A B S O L U T I S M   C U L L
R E T R A C E D   E M E N D S
    A P E D   P L A N T
R I D G E S   E L E C T R I C
A R I E L   S E A S   S Y R A
P E S   S O U R I S H   M A R
I N C H   M A I N   E L A T E
D E L U S I V E   C R A N E D
    A N I S E   S H O T
A L I G N S   S C A N T E S T
L I M E   I M P A S S I B L E
S E E R   V O I L E   C O I N
O D D S   E A T E R   E N D S
```

CROSSWORD PUZZLE NO. 2 . . . . . . page 130

```
A G A R   D O M E   M A D E   V E R B
G A V E   E V I L   O V E N   A D A R
O P A L   F I R M A M E N T   R E T E
G E L A T I N E   R E S T R A I N E D
      T I N E   G I N   S A L E
S A T I R E   A R E T E   N O D U L E
A B O V E   A R I L   R A C E   S E X
L O P E   O P E N   B R I E   W A V E
A D E   E V E N   C L O D   W A G E R
D E R I D E   A B H O R   D I V E R T
      D I R E   L I T   C E D E
P E N E T R A T E D   L A C E R A T E
I T E A   I T I N E R A T E   I R E D
C O S T   D E E D   A M E N   N E E D
A N T E   E N D S   P E R T   G A M Y
```

CROSSWORD PUZZLE NO. 3 . . . . . . page 132

```
V A L E   A S E A   A R O W   L A C E
O P E N   B A R N   Z E R O   A L A R
L E S S   A V O I D A N C E   M A S S
E X E C U T E S   E L E A   R E S E T
      O N E S   S T E W   M E N
S T A N D S   P L E A   D I S T A N T
T R I C E   H O U R   L O S T   F I R
E A S E   R E M E M B E R S   M I C E
M I L   P U L P   I O N S   F A R E S
S T E E L E D   E N D S   M I T E R S
      N O D   E R I E   I O L E
B E D E W   T E R N   U N D E R T O W
A C E R   A R R O G A N C E   N A M E
S H A G   L A I R   G A U L   A M E N
H O L Y   E Y E S   O U R S   L E N D
```

CROSSWORD PUZZLE NO. 4 . . . . . . page 134

```
C R I B   J U G G E R N A U T
R E N A   U N R E L I A B L E
E V I L   D R I N K   P L A N
D O M E   G E T S   S P E N D
I L I   G E A T   P A Y
T U T O R   D E C R Y   S I R
A T A V I C   D U O   D I M E
B I B A S I C   E N C A M P S
L O L L   G A D   G A L O R E
E N E   S A L E M   L I N E N
    H E R   V I A L   I S T
I N S E T   G I L L   C A A M
R A I A   I R A T E   A C R E
I M P R E C A T O R   R A I N
S E T T L E M E N T   P L O T
```

CROSSWORD PUZZLE NO. 5 . . . . . . page 136

```
R A J A H   T A P S   U T A H
A M U S E   O L I O   S I L O
M I D A S   K I N G   E M I L
P R Y   I C Y   E G O   E K E
      S T O O P   I N U R E S
R E P E A T   O C E A N
E V E N T   S P A S   I C E D
T E A   E P T   I T S   A V A
E R S E   R A I N   T A P E R
      R O A R S   A R D E N T
R A T I N G   M A R E S
A G E   E M U   B A N   P O E
D I R E   E S A U   G R A P E
E L S A   N E T S   T O T A L
S E E R   T R E E   H E E L S
```

CROSSWORD PUZZLE NO. 6 . . . . . . page 138

```
I M P R O M P T U   S C A R P
M E L O D I O U S   T O P E R
P R E M A T U R E   R A P P E
U R D E   E R N   S A T R A P
T I G   F R E C K L Y   O C A
E L O P E   R A N A   O V E R
S Y R I A C   P E K I N E S E
      T S A R   W E S T
S P E C T R E S   S M A R T S
C U S H   M A P S   A L E R T
R E T   M A R I T A L   F I R
A R I C I N   C A L   C U B E
P I V O T   C A T A L O G U E
P L A I T   A T O N E M E N T
Y E L L S   P E R S U A D E S
```

CROSSWORD PUZZLE NO. 7 . . . . . page 140

```
P H R A S E   S W A S T I K A
R E I N E D   H A S T E N E R
O R A T E   S A N T E E   I S
W E T S   B A N D I T   A T E
E T A   C O R N E R   K I L N
S I   C A S T O R   S A M O A
S C R A N T O N   C E R E A L
    A R D O R   H U M O R
C A N T O N   P U R P O S E S
A C T O R   C A R V E S   M U
T H E N   R O S T E R   T A B
H E R   H A L T E D   R U N T
O R   S U T L E R   C A N A L
D O M A N I A L   R O T A T E
E N A C T O R S   A B A S E R
```

CROSSWORD PUZZLE NO. 8 . . . . . page 142

```
A P P L E   S C A N   S T A R
D A R E D   C A N E   H E R O
D U E T   W A S T E   E A T S
E S S   P A R K   D R E S S Y
D E S T I N Y   S L A T E
      E N D   S E E P S   D E
S P I N S   C O A S T   H O W
W A N T   C A L L S   F I V E
A R K   B O R E S   P E T E R
M E   M O L E S   D U E
    T O N E S   W E L L O F F
S P A D E S   S E L L   R I O
C A K E   L A P E L   F A L L
A G E S   A B E D   H A T E D
R E S T   W E D S   T R E S S
```

CROSSWORD PUZZLE NO. 9 . . . . . page 144

```
A C T   E S P   P E R V A D E
W R E A T H E   S T E A R I N
R E A L T O R   A U T U M N S
Y E L L O W   O L D S   A N U
      S H A M E   O D E R
R E A C H   I R S   F L A R E
E M P H A S E S   A L E
M U T A T E D   C R O A K E D
      F E E   B E A U T I F Y
E B B E D   C A N   R E N T E
L E A S   A O R T A
O W L   O N U S   P E E V E D
P A L A V E R   P A R V E N U
E R O D E N T   E R R A N D S
R E T O R T S   W T S   A S K
```

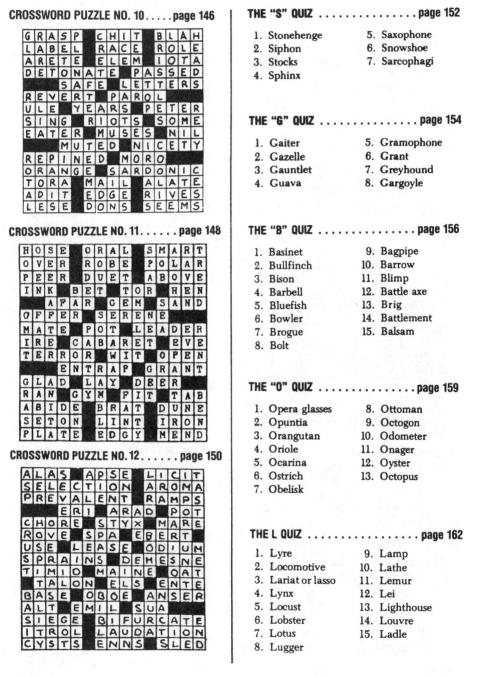

G	R	A	S	P		C	H	I	T		B	L	A	H
L	A	B	E	L		R	A	C	E		R	O	L	E
A	R	E	T	E		E	L	E	M		I	O	T	A
D	E	T	O	N	A	T	E		P	A	S	S	E	D
		S	A	F	E		L	E	T	T	E	R	S
R	E	V	E	R	T		P	A	R	O	L
U	L	E		Y	E	A	R	S		P	E	T	E	R
S	I	N	G		R	I	O	T	S		S	O	M	E
E	A	T	E	R		M	U	S	E	S		N	I	L
	M	U	T	E	D		N	I	C	E	T	Y
R	E	P	I	N	E	D		M	O	R	O
O	R	A	N	G	E		S	A	R	D	O	N	I	C
T	O	R	A		M	A	I	L		A	L	A	T	E
A	D	I	T		E	D	G	E		R	I	V	E	S
L	E	S	E		D	O	N	S		S	E	E	M	S

H	O	S	E		O	R	A	L		S	M	A	R	T
O	V	E	R		R	O	B	E		P	O	L	A	R
P	E	E	R		D	U	E	T		A	B	O	V	E
I	N	K		B	E	T		T	O	R		H	E	N
	A	F	A	R		G	E	M		S	A	N	D
O	F	F	E	R		S	E	R	E	N	E
M	A	T	E		P	O	T		L	E	A	D	E	R
I	R	E		C	A	B	A	R	E	T		E	V	E
T	E	R	R	O	R		W	I	T		O	P	E	N
	E	N	T	R	A	P		G	R	A	N	T
G	L	A	D		L	A	Y		D	E	E	R
R	A	N		G	Y	M		F	I	T		T	A	B
A	B	I	D	E		B	R	A	T		D	U	N	E
S	E	T	O	N		L	I	N	T		I	R	O	N
P	L	A	T	E		E	D	G	Y		M	E	N	D

A	L	A	S		A	P	S	E		L	I	C	I	T
S	E	L	E	C	T	I	O	N		A	R	O	M	A
P	R	E	V	A	L	E	N	T		R	A	M	P	S
	E	R	I		A	R	A	D		P	O	T
C	H	O	R	E		S	T	Y	X		M	A	R	E
R	O	V	E		S	P	A		E	B	E	R	T
U	S	E		L	E	A	S	E		O	D	I	U	M
S	P	R	A	I	N	S		D	E	M	E	S	N	E
T	I	M	I	D		M	A	I	N	E		O	A	T
	T	A	L	O	N		E	L	S		E	N	T	E
B	A	S	E		O	B	O	E		A	N	S	E	R
A	L	T		E	M	I	L		S	U	A
S	I	E	G	E		B	I	F	U	R	C	A	T	E
I	T	R	O	L		L	A	U	D	A	T	I	O	N
C	Y	S	T	S		E	N	N	S		S	L	E	D

1. Stonehenge
2. Siphon
3. Stocks
4. Sphinx
5. Saxophone
6. Snowshoe
7. Sarcophagi

1. Gaiter
2. Gazelle
3. Gauntlet
4. Guava
5. Gramophone
6. Grant
7. Greyhound
8. Gargoyle

1. Basinet
2. Bullfinch
3. Bison
4. Barbell
5. Bluefish
6. Bowler
7. Brogue
8. Bolt
9. Bagpipe
10. Barrow
11. Blimp
12. Battle axe
13. Brig
14. Battlement
15. Balsam

1. Opera glasses
2. Opuntia
3. Orangutan
4. Oriole
5. Ocarina
6. Ostrich
7. Obelisk
8. Ottoman
9. Octogon
10. Odometer
11. Onager
12. Oyster
13. Octopus

1. Lyre
2. Locomotive
3. Lariat or lasso
4. Lynx
5. Locust
6. Lobster
7. Lotus
8. Lugger
9. Lamp
10. Lathe
11. Lemur
12. Lei
13. Lighthouse
14. Louvre
15. Ladle

1. 8
2. 16
3. 55
4. 80¢
5. 8
6. 43
7. 1¼ minutes
8. 63
9. 465
10. 20
11. ⅔ hour, or 40 minutes
12. $14
13. 10½ days
14. Yes
15. Yes
16. 10 days
17. 24
18. 55 red (52 white, 47 green)
19. Pages 6, 19, and 20
20. 3 m.p.h.
21. 27
22. C = 4   5 C 4
    Y = 0   × C 5
    F = 7   ‾‾‾‾‾
    A = 2   2 F A Y
             A 1 F 6
             ‾‾‾‾‾‾‾
             A C 4 8 Y

23.   7 9 5 4
        × 6 9
       ‾‾‾‾‾‾‾
       7 1 5 8 6
       4 7 7 2 4
       ‾‾‾‾‾‾‾‾‾
       5 4 8 8 2 6

24. B = 7   C = 6   D = 4   E = 3   F = 2

1. 10	6. 8	11. 3
2. c and e	7. d	12. 2
3. a and e	8. a	13. 2
4. b and f	9. a	14. 2
5. a and e	10. c	15. 1

1.
```
4 × 4 ÷ 2 =8
×   ×   +
3 × 3 − 6 =3
÷   −   −
6 + 4 − 1 =9
=2  =8  =7
```

2.
```
5 + 9 − 8 =6
×   ×   +
3 × 2 − 4 =2
−   ÷   ÷
9 + 3 ÷ 2 =6
=6  =6  =6
```

3.
```
6 − 4 × 3 =6
×   ×   +
3 × 3 − 7 =2
÷   −   ÷
9 + 5 ÷ 2 =7
=2  =7  =5
```

4.
```
3 × 6 − 9 =9
×   +   +
3 + 7 ÷ 5 =2
−   −   ÷
2 + 9 − 7 =4
=7  =4  =2
```

247

5.

9	+	7	÷	2	=8
+		−		×	
3	×	4	−	6	=6
−				÷	
7	−	3	−	3	= 1
=5		=9		=4	

6.

6	÷	3	×	4	=8
×		+		×	
3	×	5	−	9	=6
÷		−		÷	
2	×	7	−	6	=8
=9		= 1		=6	

VOCABULARY QUIZ I . . . . page 174

page 174

1. Famous
2. Speckled
3. Talkative
4. Foreign
5. Stronghold
6. Exaggeration
7. Increase
8. Stingy
9. Ambiguous
10. Corpse
11. Hubbub
12. Row
13. Beat
14. Gap
15. Gratuity
16. Edict
17. Bulging
18. Predilection
19. Stripteaser
20. Sullen
21. Harsh

SE QUIZ . . . . page 176

page 176

1. Serve
2. Sedan
3. Sever
4. Sense
5. Sepia
6. Miser
7. Upset
8. Inset
9. Nosey
10. Asset
11. Raise
12. Lapse
13. Blase
14. Dense
15. Erase
16. Passe
17. Terse
18. Prose
19. Sabre
20. Scale
21. Skate
22. Shade
23. Spike
24. Sidle

MOVIE MEMORY . . . . page 178

page 178

1. David Niven
2. Richard Burton
3. Zero Mostel
4. Glenn Ford
5. Rod Steiger
6. Ray Milland
7. Charles Laughton
8. Joanne Woodward
9. Elizabeth Taylor
10. Michael Caine
11. Broderick Crawford
12. Lee Marvin
13. Joan Fontaine
14. Al Jolson
15. Albert Finney
16. Anthony Perkins
17. Ali MacGraw
18. Steve McQueen
19. Glenda Jackson
20. George Burns
21. Sandy Dennis
22. Paul Newman
23. Anne Bancroft
24. Diane Keaton
25. Carrie Fisher
26. Robert Redford

ON THE ROAD . . . . page 180

page 180

1. 1894
2. 50
3. $295
4. Malcolm Campbell
5. T. Roosevelt
6. Chevrolet
7. Austria
8. 17 m.p.h.
9. Gaston Chevrolet
10. $400
11. 22 feet
12. Lincoln
13. Wankel
14. Volkswagen
15. Sweden
16. Le Mans
17. 1896

18. Nicholas Cugnot
19. Radial tires
20. Tachometer
21. Volvo
22. New York Thruway
23. 15 to 1
24. Japan
25. 1903
26. Pontiac
27. Carbon monoxide
28. Carburetor

TV TEASERS

1. *Gunsmoke*
2. Los Angeles
3. 1941
4. Maynard G. Krebs
5. Sid Caesar
6. NBC
7. Ernie Kovacs
8. Broderick Crawford
9. His wife
10. Carl Betz
11. The Ponderosa
12. Paladin
13. Pancho
14. Clarabell
15. Mr. Fields
16. Paul O'Keefe
17. New York
18. Leo G. Carroll
19. Silver
20. Della Street
21. Efrem Zimbalist, Jr.
22. Buster Crabbe
23. *Jungle Jim*
24. Sapphire
25. Minneapolis
26. Barney Fife
27. Fess Parker
28. Captain Kangaroo
29. Fantasyland
30. Emmys
31. Wilma
32. Bus driver
33. Ernest Borgnine
34. Napoleon Solo

35. The final episode of *Roots*, Jan. 30, 1977
36. Eliot Ness
37. Rod Serling
38. Gomer Pyle
39. Edith
40. Harvey Korman
41. *The Defenders*
42. Dan Rowan & Dick Martin
43. Cloris Leachman
44. Opie
45. *All in the Family*

ARE YOU DECISIVE?

Part One: *Part Two:*
Group 1: D, E, G   5, 7, 9
Group 2: C, G, H   *Part Three:*
Group 3: C, G, H   2, 3

VOCABULARY QUIZ II

1. c) Blast of trumpets
2. b) Science of wines
3. c) Childish
4. c) Brilliant
5. a) Lustful
6. c) Painkiller
7. b) Secret
8. a) Brawl
9 c) Gauzy
10. b) Incisive
11. a) Praise
12. d) Charming
13. b) Essence
14. b) Habitual criminal
15. a) Unfeeling
16. c) Blunder
17. a) Outcast
18. d) Substitute
19. d) Revolutionary
20. a) Lowest point
21. a) Plunder
22. d) Sentimental
23. c) Have effect
24. b) Revoke
25. a) Journey
26. b) Continue to exist
27. d) Intruder

28. a) Omen
29. a) Shyness

DO YOU KNOW KIDS?......... page 191

1. *False* A child's brain and intelligence develop more during the years between birth and age six than during any other period in life.
2. *False* Babbling is the first experimentation with speech. The infant uses every speech sound in babbling. Ultimately the baby will retain the sounds of her own language and discard the other sounds.
3. *True* In addition, the child has reinvented complex grammatical rules and can use most parts of speech almost correctly.
4. *False* They should be given as much opportunity and space to explore as they can within the rules of safety.
5. *True* They should not be ignored. What may sound silly to you, is serious to a child. Complex questions should be answered as simply as possible. Your laughter or disinterest may stifle curiosity and cut off an important channel of learning.
6. *False* If a child shows interest, it is not wrong to try to teach him to read; but do not force a child who has not shown such a desire.
7. *False* Children learn through all five senses, but some children seem to emphasize one sense more than the others. When a baby puts objects into her mouth, worrisome as it is to parents, she is trying to learn something.
8. *False* Getting into things is not naughtiness. It is the manifestation of a natural and insatiable drive to learn.
9. *False* Toys should be creative, capable of being used in many ways. A box can be a house, a boat, car or any other wonderful thing the child decides to make it.
10. *False* The world outside the home provides many learning experiences.

Children should go to the market, shoemaker, barbershop with parents. They should meet people outside the family. However, plan your trips so they will be short and still leave time for you to give your child enough attention.

PRESIDENTIAL PRECEDENTS ..... page 192

1. d. Andrew Jackson g. 1828
2. c. Tyler (He had 8 children with his first wife, and 7 with his second.)
3. a. Hoover (He died at 90.)
4. a. Lincoln, Nebraska
   b. Jefferson City, Missouri
   c. Madison, Wisconsin
   d. Jackson, Mississippi
5. a. William Harrison
   b. Zachary Taylor
   c. Warren Harding
   d. Franklin D. Roosevelt
6. a. Abraham Lincoln
   b. James Garfield
   c. William McKinley
   d. John Kennedy
7. b. Coolidge (1872)
8. j. Adams and Jefferson (1826)
9. d. Lincoln (6'4") g. Madison (5'4")
10. a. Abigail Smith (Adams)
11. d. Tyler
12. a. 1932   Herbert Hoover
    b. 1936   Alfred Landon
    c. 1940   Wendell Willkie
    d. 1944   Thomas Dewey
13. c. Johnson
14. d. Washington (1793)
15. c. Wilson (1920)
16. c. F.D. Roosevelt (1933)

GRAB BAG................. page 194

1. d) Brazil
2. b) Thelma
3. c) Alfred Tennyson
4. a) Poseidon
5. c) David Janssen
6. d) Corned beef and swiss cheese
7. a) 1914

8. b) California
9. b) Quintuplets
10. a) Dust Commander
11. c) 39
12. b) 50,000 sq. mi.
13. b) Fennel
14. b) Apples
15. c) George Eastman
16. b) Olympia
17. b) 1945
18. b) 11
19. b) Lew Alcindor
20. b) Ulysses S.Grant
21. c) A dessert
22. b) Darling

ARE YOU WELL-READ? . . . . page 196

1. *Othello*
2. *Lorna Doone*
3. *Ben-Hur*
4. *Crime and Punishment*
5. *The Naked and the Dead*
6. T. S. Eliot
7. Jim
8. *Jude the Obscure*
9. 22 Baker Street
10. Jean Valjean
11. *Orlando*
12. *Robinson Crusoe*
13. William Wilkie Collins
14. Ralph Ellison
15. *Nana*
16. James Barrie
17. 3 parts
18. *Miss Julie*
19. Don Quixote
20. Geoffrey Chaucer
21. Captain Nemo
22. Becky Sharp
23. Poem
24. Joseph Heller
25. *Clea*

IN OTHER WORDS. . . . . page 198

1. A rolling stone gathers no moss.
2. Too many cooks spoil the broth.

3. People who live in glass houses should never throw stones.
4. The early bird catches the worm.
5. All that glitters is not gold.
6. Waste not, want not.
7. A fool and his money are soon parted.
8. 'Tis an ill wind that blows no good.
9. Look before you leap
10. To err is human; to forgive, divine.
11. It's no use crying over spilled milk.
12. The squeaky wheel gets the most oil.
13. You can catch more flies with honey than with vinegar.
14. There's no fool like an old fool.
15. You can't teach an old dog new tricks.
16. A watched pot never boils.

CHECKLIST FOR THE LITERATI . . . . page 200

1. To depart this life
2. Between two dangers, neither of which can be avoided
3. To cleverly give a dexterous turn to a situation
4. A burdensome possession
5. To give alarm without occasion
6. An illusion of plenty
7. To admonish with severity and directness
8. Things affectedly despised because they cannot be possessed
9. To be rolling in riches
10. Poignant, delicate wit
11. To dispose of a difficulty by prompt, arbitrary action
12. A cruel taskmaster
13. To fight imaginary enemies
14. An absurd belief
15. To go without dinner
16. Of imperial birth
17. To squander foolishly
18. Stirring up or reviving sectional animosity
19. A victory gained at too great cost
20. To follow policies which will lead to war
21. Dilatory tactics calculated to wear out the enemy
22. Something whose true value is unknown

251

QUIET ON THE SET! . . . . page 203

1. Ingmar Bergman
2. Victor Fleming
3. Robert Altman
4. Lina Wertmuller
5. Alfred Hitchcock
6. Federico Fellini
7. Woody Allen
8. Peter Bogdanovich
9. Franco Zeffirelli
10. Milos Forman
11. Billy Wilder
12. George Roy Hill
13. George Cukor
14. Hal Ashby
15. Ken Russell
16. Frank Capra
17. Howard Hawks
18. Joseph Losey
19. Sergio Leone
20. D.W. Griffith
21. Sidney Lumet
22. George Lucas
23. Laurence Olivier
24. Orson Welles
25. Cecil B. DeMille
26. Michael Curtiz
27. Joseph Mankiewicz
28. Henri Costa-Gavras
29. Robert Wise
30. Stephen Spielberg
31. William Friedkin
32. Fritz Lang
33. Pier Paolo Pasolini
34. Howard Hawks
35. Martin Scorcese
36. Stanley Kubrick
37. Stephen Spielberg
38. Nicholas Ray
39. Victor Fleming
40. William Friedkin

DO YOU KNOW FOOD? . . . . page 206

1. Lasagna
2. Feijoada completa
3. Coddled egg
4. Raw fish
5. Green noodles
6. Spiciness
7. With ice cream
8. German salami
9. Dessert pancakes
10. Mulligatawny
11. Meat pies
12. Dolmadas
13. Beef stroganoff
14. Rijsttafel
15. Low calorie
16. Goulash
17. Doused in cognac and ignited

COMMANDER-IN-CHIEF . . . . page 208

1. John Quincy Adams was elected president in 1824 and served one term; he served nine terms in the House beginning in 1831.
2. Teddy Roosevelt
3. Franklin D. Roosevelt
4. Herbert Hoover
5. Thomas Jefferson
6. John C. Calhoun, in 1832
7. Franklin D. Roosevelt. Calvin Coolidge, a Republican, was elected Warren Harding's vice-president in 1920 and succeeded to the presidency on Harding's death in 1923. He was reelected in 1924.
8. William Howard Taft
9. William Henry Harrison, after being president only 31 days, in 1840.
10. Andrew Jackson
11. Warren G. Harding, in 1920.
12. 1840, with the election of William Henry Harrison; the coincidence has continued through the presidencies of Lincoln (elected 1860), Garfield (elected 1880), McKinley (1900), Harding (1920), Roosevelt (1940), and Kennedy (1960).
13. James Madison, in August of 1814.
14. Teddy Roosevelt was 42 when he was sworn in to succeed the deceased McKinley in September of 1901. John Kennedy was 43 at the time of his election in 1960.
15. 4 presidents. Lincoln (April 4, 1865), Garfield (July 2, 1881), McKinley (September 6, 1901), and Kennedy (November 22, 1963).

16. Warren G. Harding
17. The Populist Party (Federalist presidents elected include Washington; and Whig presidents include Harrison).
18. Eisenhower (Alaska and Hawaii both joined in 1959).
19. Woodrow Wilson married his second wife in 1915, while serving his first term.
20. Virginia (birthplace of presidents Washington, Jefferson, Madison, Monroe, Harrison, Tyler, Taylor, and Wilson); in second place is Ohio, which has borne 7.

PRATFALL . . . . page 211

Merrily do I on haystacks cavort; no risk to my bottom in this kind of sport.

HEADSTRONG . . . . page 211

The mind is its own place, and in itself can make a heaven of hell, a hell of heaven.
John Milton, *Paradise Lost*

FAREWELL, FALSE LOVER . . . . . . page 212

I'm through with your promises
    and with your kisses,
Until you are through with your
    Janes and Melissas.

FEARFUL, TEARFUL . . . . page 212

The difficult child is the child who is unhappy. He is at war with himself and in consequence he is at war with the world.
A. S. Neill

QUEER BIRD . . . . page 213

My quest for quetzal fulfilled. Have my quota of quarry. Now fear quarantine.
Quaveringly,
Queenie

FOR LOVE OF LIFE . . . . page 214

The biophilous person is attracted by the very process of life, and by growth of every manner. He prefers structure to summation.
Erich Fromm

OH FICKLE FLAME . . . . page 215

The only difference between a caprice and a lifelong passion is that the caprice lasts a little longer.
Oscar Wilde, *The Picture of Dorian Gray*

ANGLOPHILIA . . . . page 215

Whan a man is tired of London, he is tired of life; for there is in London all that life can afford.
Boswell's Life of Dr. Johnson

HUMOR US . . . . page 216

No man who has once heartily and wholly laughed can be altogether irreclaimably bad.
Thomas Carlyle, Sartor Resartus

DIVINE DETERMINATION . . . . page 216

Dapper, daring, dynamic, deft, dogged daredevil delivers dainty damsel from dread danger. Dashing, doughty dude disdains dough; demands devotion.

EVIL IS LIVE BACKWARDS . . . . page 217

From the mountains of Butte, Montana came Robert Craig Knievel, daredevil stunt rider who to dramatize his billing chose the nickname Evel.
Incredible Athletic Feats

MAIN STREET............... page 218

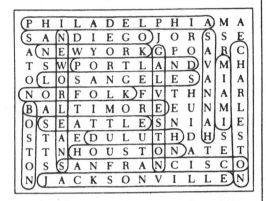

SECRET MESSAGE: *Major seaports of the United States*

FEATHERED FRIENDS .... page 220

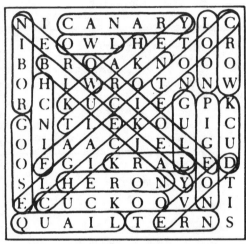

BE A SPORT................ page 219

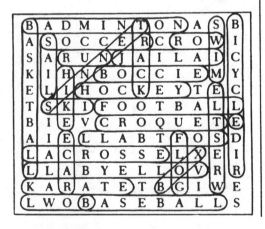

SECRET WORD: *Activities*

VEGETABLE STEW .... page 221

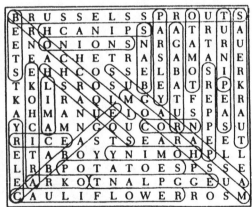